The 1931 Massie-Kahahawai case, ...~.....g a ...~~ accusation of rape followed by the killing of an accused assailant, laid bare the race-based fractures in Hawai'i society. In *What We Must Remember*, a group of poets "talk story," speaking in the voices of the varied participants in the events. In the verse documentary tradition of Stephen Vincent Benét's epic "John Brown's Body" and Anna Deavere Smith's plays, this book is a stirring work that uses art to unlock the story of a searing event in American history.

—**Greg Robinson**
Département d'Histoire
Université du Québec À Montréal

There are many accounts of the infamous Massie Case, rendered in pamphlets, essays, documentary film, a TV miniseries, a play, an opera, and books by novelists, journalists, and historians. Almost all these works were produced by *haole*, most by people who never lived in Hawai'i. Of necessity, they were on the outside looking in. Missing was a pathway to the inside. *What We Must Remember* is a meditation and exchange among four local poets, exploring through "documentary *renshi*" the imagined consciousness of victimizers and victims, observers and observed. It is a fresh and emotionally engaging piece of work.

—**David E. Stannard**
Author of *Honor Killing: How the Infamous*
"Massie Affair" Transformed Hawai'i

What We Must Remember is above all a highly nuanced *renshi* that blends the work of four accomplished poets into a moving response to one of the most notorious and culturally significant moments in Hawaii's history. But this collection is also a valuable archive, providing readers with historical background and references for further study and including fascinating and informative essays by the poets themselves about the process of collaborative composition for the entire *renshi*, as well as for each of their individual links. Many have told us about the Massie-Kahahawai cases; *What We Must Remember* guides us in how to feel about them.

—**Craig Howes**
Director, Center for Biographical Research
University of Hawai'i at Mānoa

The four skilled *renshi* poets and authors of *What We Must Remember* revisit and revision one of the most disturbing episodes in Territorial Hawai'i. The Massie-Kahāhāwai case was disruptive on many levels—legal, social, personal, local, and national. The details were documented in the day through layers of news, story, and memory and the well-informed poets make the historical fresh again through their lyrics and narratives. The poetry is compelling and experiential; events are viewed through multiple, overlapping perspectives, the spin and eddy of each section being like shards of a broken mirror. The essays illuminate both the events and the processes of bringing them into new form. It is a powerful way to reflect.

—**Puakea Nogelmeier**
Professor of Hawaiian Language
University of Hawai'i at Mānoa

Important, unique, and timely, this book of poems, with illuminating commentary on the process of its making, asks of history: *what must we remember?* In this sensitive reconstruction of racist crime and official injustice, giving voice to those involved, four poets choose to link their poems, creating unexpected discoveries as they imaginatively enter together one of the uglier chapters of Hawaii's history. A moving exploration of the human cost of privileged prejudice, and how collaborative creative process can reveal it.

—**Eleanor Wilner**
Author of *The Girl with Bees in Her Hair*

What We Must Remember

What We Must Remember

LINKED POEMS

Christy Passion
Ann Inoshita
Juliet S. Kono
Jean Yamasaki Toyama

BAMBOO RIDGE PRESS

ISBN 978-0-910043-97-7

This is issue #111 (Spring 2017) of *Bamboo Ridge, Journal of Hawai'i Literature and Arts* (ISSN 0733-0308)

Published by Bamboo Ridge Press
Printed in the United States of America

Indexed in *Humanities International Complete*

Bamboo Ridge Press is a member of the Community of Literary Magazines and Presses (CLMP).

Typesetting and design: Jui-Lien Sanderson
Photos of Juliet S. Kono and Jean Yamasaki Toyama by Jui-Lien Sanderson
Photo of Ann Inoshita by Rowen Tabusa
Photos of Christy Passion and John P. Rosa courtesy of authors

Cover images courtesy of the Hawai'i State Archives, the Honolulu Police Department Museum,
and the *Honolulu Star-Advertiser*.

Bamboo Ridge Press is a nonprofit, tax-exempt corporation formed in 1978 to foster the appreciation,
understanding, and creation of literary, visual, or performing arts by, for, or about Hawaii's people. This
publication was made possible with support from the Hawai'i Council for the Humanities, the National
Endowment for the Arts (NEA), and the Hawai'i State Foundation on Culture and the Arts (SFCA),
through appropriations from the Legislature of the State of Hawai'i (and grants by the NEA).

Bamboo Ridge is published twice a year. For subscription information, back issues, or a catalog,
please contact:

Bamboo Ridge Press
P.O. Box 61781,
Honolulu, HI 96839-1781
808.626.1481
brinfo@bambooridge.com
www.bambooridge.com

...this is a tale of unfaltering courage by a few in the face of overwhelming intimidation. However much it is rooted in the past, it is a story with a powerful message for the present.

David E. Stannard
Honor Killing

CONTENTS
▼ ▼ ▼

Introduction

What We Must Remember is a work of literature inspired by historical events that took place more than eighty years ago. Instead of being a standard historical account, it is a collaborative, linked poem about the Massie-Kahahawai case of 1931–1932, undertaken by four poets: Christy Passion, Ann Inoshita, Juliet S. Kono, and Jean Yamasaki Toyama. Beginning in 2011, I took part in discussions about their *renshi* in progress and accompanied them at forums, including the Hawai'i Book and Music Festival in Honolulu and the national conference of the Association for Asian American Studies in Seattle. They had asked me to provide an overview of the case so that those unfamiliar with it and the history of Hawai'i could better understand references in their work. And so, let us begin by recounting the events.

After a lively Saturday night in Waikīkī, Thalia Massie, a twenty-year-old white woman married to Thomas Massie, a twenty-six-year-old naval officer stationed at Pearl Harbor, said that she had been raped by a group of Hawaiians in the early morning hours of Sunday, September 13, 1931. That night Thalia admitted to police that she could not see her assailants' faces, but within a couple of days, she identified five young men who were brought before her and subsequently charged with her assault. All were in their early twenties and had known each other since their days at Kauluwela Elementary School and sports activities in the Kalihi-Pālama area. Joseph Kahahawai and Ben Ahakuelo were Native Hawaiians, well known for their skills in barefoot football and boxing. Horace Ida and David Takai were from the Japanese community that then made up over forty percent of the islands' population. And Henry Chang was Hawaiian and Chinese—a person of mixed ancestry, not uncommon in multiethnic Hawai'i.

The five working-class, "local" youths were tried for the rape of Thalia Massie in the *Territory of Hawaii v. Ahakuelo, et al.* The trial was covered extensively in the islands by *The Honolulu Advertiser* and *Honolulu Star-Bulletin* as well as by the Japanese language newspapers, the *Hawaii Hochi* and *Nippu Jiji*, and Hawaiian language newspapers like the *Ke Alakai o Hawaii* and *Ka Hoku o Hawaii*. Due to a lack of firm evidence and contradictory testimony, the jury was unable to reach a verdict after 97 hours of deliberation. The judge declared a mistrial, but before a second trial could be convened, two incidents of vigilantism occurred. Horace Ida was kidnapped from a speakeasy in downtown Honolulu in December 1931 by a group of Navy men who beat him and threatened to throw him over the Nu'uanu Pali if he did not confess to the alleged rape of Thalia Massie. Local newspapers published photos of Ida's back bruised from being beaten and whipped with belts. And then on the morning of January 8, 1932, Joseph Kahahawai was kidnapped from the steps of Ali'iolani Hale, the court building where the young men had been reporting daily as a condition of their bail.

Thalia Massie's mother, Grace Fortescue, her husband Thomas, and Edward Lord and Albert Jones, two Navy men hired by the family, had abducted Joseph Kahahawai. At about 8:15 a.m., they had lured him closer to their car with a fake summons, pushed him into the vehicle, and had driven him to Fortescue's rented home in Mānoa where they tried to coerce a confession out of him. When Joe refused to admit to raping Thalia—something he emphatically said he did not do— he was shot in the heart and bled to death.

With Kahahawai's body in the back seat, Grace Fortescue drove the Massies' Buick sedan to Halona Blowhole near Hanauma Bay. They hoped the ocean would wash evidence of their guilt away, but the Honolulu Police Department had already been alerted with a description of the car by Joe's cousin who saw the kidnapping. The police chased their car all the way to the Halona Lookout and caught the Massie-Fortesue group red-handed. They found the body in the car in a large laundry basket, wrapped in a bed sheet.

In the murder trial of *Territory v. Massie, Fortescue, Lord, and Jones*, the famous Clarence Darrow was hired to defend the Massie-Fortescue group, a far cry from his reputation as being an "attorney for the damned" and an advocate for the working class. A much younger territorial prosecutor, John Kelley, defeated Darrow in court; then a jury of twelve local men found the group guilty of the lesser charge of manslaughter. Though the jury recommended leniency, Judge Charles Davis sentenced Fortescue, Thomas Massie, Lord, and Jones to ten years hard labor at Oahu Prison. In a remarkable twist, however, the group was marched across King Street downtown to the governor's office at 'Iolani Palace. There,

Territorial Governor Lawrence McCully Judd commuted their sentences to a mere hour in his office, where they drank tea, some say, or even champagne. They left the islands a few days later with the assistance of the Navy, never to return. By the end of the spring 1932, national attention had already shifted to the gripping news story of the kidnapping of aviator Charles Lindbergh's baby son. For most on the continental United States, the tale of the Massie-Kahahawai case was quickly and easily forgotten. But in the islands, it was anything but so.

When people hear of the Massie-Kahahawai case for the first time, they often cannot believe it is a true story, not a work of fiction. Because of its myriad of details, many turn to books, articles, videos, and other works that recount or are inspired by the historical events. (See the timeline that follows and suggestions for further reading and viewing at the end of this book for more information.) As important as they are, instead of focusing solely on the details of the case, let us consider for a moment the interrelationship of *story*, *memory*, and *history*. Collectively, all three are part of a *shared culture*—something living and continually in the making—formed by individuals and communities over the course of multiple generations. As part of this process, stories are circulated, memories are formed, and histories are written and published.

With the Massie-Kahahawai case, people *talked story* about it in the early 1930s as it unfolded. They discussed the interrelated rape and murder trials among themselves in their communities, often informed by, or in opposition to, newspaper accounts in the islands and on the continental U.S. Multiple stories circulated in various genres. For many on the continent, it was merely a sensational true crime story that splashed the pages of newspapers and popular magazines. For those in the islands, however, the case resonated with neighborhoods and families on a personal level. Because of the racial and ethnic backgrounds of the accused, the case was extensively discussed in the Native Hawaiian and local Japanese communities. The fact that one of the accused, Henry Chang, was of mixed Chinese and Hawaiian ancestry also made the story one about interracial mixing and demographic change in the islands that were uncommon elsewhere on the continental U.S. where interracial marriage was rare, and in some states, illegal.

After a few years, stories about the Massie-Kahahawai case were rarely shared in public. They entered into the realm of *memory*. These storied accounts were kept closely by individuals related to the case or those who had read about it first-hand in newspapers during the early 1930s. For the next two decades, the case was almost never discussed, partly because during the World War II years and Cold War era, it was difficult to talk openly about racial tensions between Hawai'i residents and the military, between the Territory of Hawaii and the federal government. To do so would be seen as unpatriotic and un-American. It might surprise some today that the case was not always openly discussed. Similar in some ways as a historical injustice to the overthrow of the Hawaiian Kingdom or Japanese American internment during World War II, the events of the Massie case were frequently seen as too painful to bring up, let alone critically address. There was too much hurt, too much pain and raw emotion, for communities at large and for families related to those in the case, even decades after the initial events had transpired.

Though labor activist John Reinecke published an account of the case in 1950 (drawing parallels to the Majors-Palakiko case), there were no more publications about it until the mid-1960s. Three books appeared in 1966, mainly in the vein of "true crime" accounts. For better or for worse, these were the first thorough, written histories of the case, albeit without the strictures of footnotes and other academic conventions. Nevertheless, they were carefully researched at what is now the Hawai'i State Archives. It wasn't until the late 1960s and the 1970s that mention of the Massie-Kahahawai case appeared in print in the islands again in newspaper retrospectives and college curricula. By the 1980s and 1990s, textbook accounts of the case and other published materials were being used not only by university students but high school students studying the history of Hawai'i. A larger public also became aware of the case through the highly fictionalized novel by Norman Katov that was later turned into the 1986 CBS television mini-series *Blood and Orchids*.

By the turn of the 21st century, greater awareness of the Massie-Kahahawai case had gained momentum. A number of writers and scholars researched the case with fresh eyes and a popular storyteller, Glen Grant, armed with a PhD in American studies, was giving tours about it at Aliʻiolani Hale, the very court building in which the rape and murder trials took place. In 2001, *The Honolulu Advertiser* published a short piece by David Stannard asking local readers to share their stories about the case for the book he was working on. Well-known newspaper reporter Cobey Black was also finally able to publish *Hawaii Scandal* (Island Heritage, 2002), her book that had been delayed for over three decades because too many books were published about the case in 1966.

As for the book that you currently have in your hands, the *renshi* poets asked me for a professional historian's commentary while they were revising their drafts, as I was completing my own book, *Local Story: The Massie-Kahahawai Case and the Culture of History* (University of Hawaiʻi Press, 2014). Christy, Ann, Juliet, and Jean were using another work published in the 21st century as part of their writing process: University of Hawaiʻi American Studies Professor David Stannard's *Honor Killing: How the Infamous "Massie Affair" Transformed Hawaiʻi* (Penguin Group, 2005). For the facts of the case, the poets primarily drew upon their reading of *Honor Killing*. At nearly 500 pages, it is a rich history of territorial Hawaiʻi with enough room for Stannard to lay out his carefully researched prose account that explains the major and minor players in the case and the history of the territorial period. These academic monographs by Professor Stannard and myself are only two cultural productions about the Massie-Kahahawai case to see the light of day in the 21st century. In 2005, filmmaker Mark Zwonitzer released *The Massie Affair*, a one-hour PBS documentary produced by WGBH Boston as part of its American Experience series. One year earlier, Kumu Kahua Theatre had an extremely successful run of *Massie/Kahahawai*, a Brechtian play that University of Hawaiʻi Theater Professor Dennis Carroll wrote in the late 1960s and early 1970s, but did not stage at the time due to threats of lawsuits by Thomas Massie, who was still alive in San Diego at the time.

Carroll had painstakingly pieced together text from various newspaper accounts, police records, and other sources in order to create his play. In the last decade or so, other artists like Hawaiʻi poet Gizelle Gajelonia and photographer Jan Becket have also produced works related to the Massie-Kahahawai case. Though the *renshi* poets sometimes said that they momentarily felt "constrained by actual events" during the writing process, it was the historical realities of the case that inspired them to think deeply and reimagine what it might have been like to live in territorial Hawai'i, a place that was both politically disempowered and more racially charged than today. Nearly each poet said that she inhabited the skin of a different, real life individual in the case at some point. In one instance, even the green dress worn by Thalia Massie and referenced to in both the rape and murder trials as an item of evidence took on a vital voice.

"History" will always have its problems and complexities. It is flawed. It can be incomplete. And it often fails to record the emotions of individuals, families, and communities who have been directly impacted by historical events. Properly speaking, this *renshi* is not a history but a communal work and part of our collective local culture that links us (both as poets and readers) to the Massie-Kahahawai case and its ongoing legacy. History, after all, is a dialogue between past and present. And Hawaii's history is anything but distant to us. We are reminded of the Massie-Kahahawai case through generations of telling and retelling stories. Now we are no longer forgetting but remembering our shared history. And to remember is more than just to call to mind. It is to re-member, to put pieces together in an attempt to make things whole.

John P. Rosa
Associate Professor of History
University of Hawai'i at Mānoa

Timeline

1931

September 12–13

Late Saturday night / early Sunday morning in Waikīkī enjoyed by locals and military personnel.

Police report of alleged rape of Thalia Massie by Ben Ahakuelo, Henry Chang, Horace Ida, Joseph Kahahawai, and David Takai.

September 14–15

Honolulu police question possible suspects. Ben Ahakuelo, Henry Chang, Horace Ida, Joseph Kahahawai, and David Takai are charged with the assault of Thalia Massie.

November 18–December 6

Territory of Hawaii v. Ahakuelo et al. trial for the alleged rape of Thalia Massie. A jury of local men (1 haole, 1 Portuguese, 6 part-Hawaiians, 2 Japanese, and 2 Chinese) deliberates for 97 hours and is unable to agree on a verdict. It ends in a mistrial.

December 13

Horace Ida is beaten by Navy men.

1932

January 8

Joseph Kahahawai is abducted by Thalia Massie's mother, Grace Fortescue; her husband, Thomas Massie; and two Navy men, Edward Lord and Albert "Deacon" Jones. They try to coerce a confession but Kahahawai refuses to admit to the rape and is killed. Massie subsequently admits in court that he pulled the trigger but many years later, Jones says that he was actually the one who shot Kahahawai.

January 10

Kahahawai's funeral. *Honolulu Star-Bulletin* reports two thousand in attendance.

April 11–29
Territory of Hawaii v. Massie, Fortescue, Lord, and Jones trial for the murder of Joseph Kahahawai.

May 4
Guilty verdict for the lesser charge of manslaughter for Grace Fortescue, Thomas Massie, Edward Lord, and Albert Jones. Judge Charles Davis sentences the group to ten years at hard labor. Less than one hour later, Territorial Governor Lawrence McCully Judd commutes (shortens) their sentences to one hour at his office in ʻIolani Palace.

October
Pinkerton Detective Agency Report delivers report to Governor Judd. Concludes there is no major evidence to show that Ahakuelo, Ida, Takai, Chang, and Kahahawai committed assault on Thalia Massie.

1951
Majors-Palakiko case prompts the *Honolulu Record* to issue a pamphlet on the Massie case authored anonymously by John Reinecke.

1963
Thalia Massie commits suicide in West Palm Beach, Florida, overdosing on barbiturates.

1966
Publication of 3 books on the case: Theon Wright's *Rape in Paradise*, Peter Van Slingerland's *Something Terrible Has Happened*, and Robert Packer and Bob Thomas's *The Massie Case*.

1967
Former Governor Judd tells the *Honolulu Star-Bulletin* that he "acted under the heaviest pressure" in commuting the Massie-Fortescue group's sentences and worried that the Territory of Hawaii would have been put under a commission

form of government administered by the U.S. Navy if the defendants had to serve their sentences of hard labor.

1968
Ben Ahakuelo becomes the first and only of the five suspects to grant a newspaper interview.

1986
Television miniseries *Blood and Orchids* airs on CBS.

1988–1996
Glen Grant offers monthly tours focusing on the Massie case.

2001
University of Hawai'i American studies professor David Stannard issues a call for stories about the Massie-Kahahawai case through *The Honolulu Advertiser*.

2002
Cobey Black's book, *Hawaii Scandal*, is published by Island Heritage.

2004
Dennis Carroll's play, *Massie/Kahahawai*, runs at Kumu Kahua Theatre.

2005
David Stannard's book, *Honor Killing*, and Mark Zwonitzer's *American Experience* documentary, *The Massie Affair*, are released in April.

2010
Poet Gizelle Gajelonia publishes a poem about the Massie case in her chapbook, *Thirteen Ways of Looking at TheBus* (Honolulu: Tinfish Press).

2011–2013
Four Bamboo Ridge poets, Christy Passion, Ann Inoshita, Juliet S. Kono, and Jean

Yamasaki Toyama, compose a *renshi* (linked poem) from August 2011 to May 2012. Parts of the *renshi* are presented at the Hawai'i Book and Music Festival in 2012 and at the national conference of the Association for Asian American Studies in Seattle in 2013.

2012

The *Hawaii Independent*, an online news source, commemorates the death of Joseph Kahahawai 80 years before.

2014

John Rosa's *Local Story: The Massie-Kahahawai Case and the Culture of History* is published by University of Hawai'i Press.

2016

Craig Howes, Jon Kamakawiwo'ole Osorio, and John Rosa of the University of Hawai'i are interviewed about the case for a 2017 television episode of *A Crime to Remember*. Carol Maxym announces in the *Honolulu Star-Advertiser* that she is developing an opera based on the events of the Massie-Kahahawai case.

Honolulu Civil Beat and PRX radio produce a 10-part podcast series on race and federal power in Hawai'i. It compares the Massie case to the Christopher Deedy case in which a federal agent shot a young Native Hawaiian man, Kollin Elderts in Waikīkī in 2011, shortly before the opening of the Asia-Pacific Economic Cooperation (APEC) Leaders' Meeting with more than 20 heads of state in attendance.

Prologue

A Cautionary Tale

Riding on the success of *No Choice but to Follow* (Bamboo Ridge Press, 2010), we *renshi* poets wanted to do something, but something different. At Juliet's suggestion, we started a new *renshi* based on the actual events of the infamous "Massie Case." Once again, we revealed each poem on the Bamboo Ridge Press website, beginning at the end of August 2011. Instead of one week (as in our previous project) we gave each other two weeks to write and post each link, using the last line of the preceding poem as our title. The order would be reversed; this time Christy would be first and Jean last.

The year 2011 marked the 80th anniversary of the Massie case, but except for Juliet, we didn't have anything but the vaguest notion about these events. We needed to learn the facts and understand the times. Later we learned of "documentary poetry" and concluded that ours was a "documentary *renshi*." It sounded right because we were going to write links about events that actually happened.

After ten months we stopped. In spite of the flow of creative energy, we found the experience emotionally draining. We literally abandoned the project.

The events of the intervening five years, especially 2016, breathed new life into our effort. We felt an urgency to complete this work. We did not want to be condemned for our forgetfulness, as surely George Santayana would have. We earnestly hoped not to join "those who cannot remember the past [and] are condemned to repeat it."

Thus came our title: *What We Must Remember*. Our *renshi* speaks of the times, past and present.

In retrospect, this project was an ambitious undertaking, one that we took on blindly. For some reason we had no fear. As it turned out, what we covered was but a tiny portion of what occurred. Of course, we never realistically believed that we could cover everything. What we did achieve, though, was something different and unique. We gave voice to those who are usually written about, who do not usually speak: the jurors, the spectators, the Admiral, the two mothers, Thalia's friend, even the dress. You will hear their voices in our *renshi*.

Can something of value be added to our collective remembrance, something that would be worth the pain? The answer lies in your hands.

The Poems

Reading Assignment: Stannard's *Honor Killing*

I don't want to read this story.

Don't want to know their names, imagine their faces.

I catch my breath as the words surface:
Tin Can Alley, bare feet football,
brown-skinned boys wearing white silk shirts.
See them behind the wheel—immortal for the night;
hear the ease in their laughter
stronger than daylight and the poor.

Too close to home.

It is my father's stories of his Hawai'i.
There were few comforts, but
there were dances at the Ala Wai Club,
Violet's in Kalihi—stew bowl for 25 cents,
there were beatings, Japs, Haoles, Blahlaz, and curfew;
dirty cops way too willing, rats that climbed up
tin gutters, girls with nice legs who gave it up
easy, and if you were lucky, real lucky,
a job at the shipyard.

Was different back den Chris
no can believe, was so hard. But we work,
go drink, talk story, forget for little while

This is not Michener's Hawai'i.

I skip to the end where she commits suicide—
and like a child burning ants, feel

a false sense of power. The end gathers me up
for the journey back.

This story is the unwanted family heirloom
the ugly vase,
the chipped china,
the bastard child everyone whispers about,
but no one calls by name.

—Christy Passion

One Call: Sunday, September 13, 1931

Saturday night wasn't busy in the Kapi'olani building,
so no one from the Honolulu police could predict
an early morning phone call
that changed Hawai'i forever.

Before the call came, Agnes Peeples
walked into the building at 12:45 a.m.
Agnes said her husband was driving
when they encountered a car filled with men
where King and Liliha intersect.

Although the cars didn't hit,
Agnes and a man from the other car fought,
resulting in blood seeping from her ear.
She remembered the car's license number: 58-985,
and Officer Cecil Rickard recorded her statement.

The phone rings at 1:47 a.m.,
so Captain Hans Kashiwabara picks up.
Tommie Massie reports an assault
and wants the police to visit his house.

The captain calls Detective John Jardine.
Then Jardine contacts Rickard
who instructs police to drive to the Massie home.

Detective Harbottle, Detective Furtado, and Officer Simerson
listen as Thalia Massie speaks:

She was at the Ala Wai Inn
and went for a walk at about midnight
when a car with four or five Hawaiians came by.

She was forced into the car and punched.
They drove her to a secluded area,
removed her from the car to the bushes,
and raped her six or seven times.

—Ann Inoshita

They Raped Her

she alleged, six or seven times
in her beautiful green dress.
I was that green dress.

Now,
I am the ghost
of that green dress.
These days,
I float ethereally,
from where the Ala Wai Inn stood,
down to John Ena Road
near Fort DeRussy,
where Mrs. George Goeas,
Alice Araki, and Eugenio Batungbacal
testified they saw me pass by,
which places me
in the area late that night.

I am the ghost of the green dress Thalia
wore when she said she was abducted
by five "Hawaiians"
and brought to a place,
dark, isolated, desolate,
in Ala Moana
known as Beach Road,
where only a few
small fishing boats
creaked in darkness
and dogs whined,
their cries coming from the old
animal quarantine station.

I am the ghost of the dress
that continues to weave in and out
of the psyche of Hawaii's people.
Then again that's another story.

I am the ghost of the green dress,
iridescent as the ocean
when in the limu's green-bloom,
a green that accentuated
the color of her fair skin
her light, soulful eyes,
rose-pink lips,
and fine brown hair.
To have seen her,
you would have been
hard-pressed to say
she was pretty;
but unconventionally
attractive, she was taller
than most women in the islands
and had a kind of lugubrious
chicness made of old money
and deep unhappiness,
as she walked away from the Inn
in an inebriated sway.

In the car
where she said she was raped,
I don't remember
if I was lifted gently from her legs
or shoved up to her waist
with trembling hands
or pressed by desire

against the heaving
want and weight
of desperate men.
I don't remember if they nestled
their need into my neckline
as they drooled into her cleavage,
if indeed, they even did.

After whatever happened,
once at home,
I was taken off
and hung like a scarecrow
in her bedroom.
She called the police
to say she'd been beaten
and raped and the detectives
came to take her statement,
but Detective Bill Furtado
and his partner, George Harbottle,
did not inspect me much,
as I swayed in winds from the valley.

Only later was I scrutinized,
whereupon they found but a tiny blood
spot and bit of soil. Nothing more.
I remained green, was clean.

I don't know when it happened,
this part folded into my imagination.
But some months later, *if ever*,
I was stripped from the hanger,
and stomped on, in anger.
Torn from across the bodice,

I was dragged out,
taken to the backyard,
where I was hung and set on fire.
Burned in effigy.

—Juliet S. Kono

Burned in Effigy

"It ain't in effigy I wanna burn 'em
but in the flesh, real bones, covered in dark skins.
The papers didn't give her name, jus' said 'a beautiful
young woman, cultured and of gentle bearing.' For
sure she was white and raped. We wouldn't stand for
that where I come from."

That's what my buddy said.
Maybe he's right.

My own blood boiled seeing them
black boys right on top—on top, mind you—
of white girls.
Even on surfboards it still ain't right,
skin on skin.
On the beach they're laughin'
strummin' ukuleles, singin', smilin',
oh, yes, smilin'.

And then those colored girls here
don't act polite. You say hello, they look
right through you like you not even there.
At home no girl treated me that way.
This ain't no dreamy Hawai'i,
no joy zone. The movies lie.
Things ain't right here. Color'ds
don't know their place.

We heard the Admiral called them rapists,
sordid people, brutes and hoodlums.
Two of them are even from that orange race,
the one they say we gonna fight one day.

My buddy told me I jus' had no guts because
I didn't wanna go down to the jail to burn 'em.
Then he shoves the paper in my face, "Read those names.
Ida, Chang, Kahahawai, Takai, Ahakuelo.
What are they? Not American."

—Jean Yamasaki Toyama

What Are They

I said nothing
the night they came, the first night gone

put away the stew warming on the stove,
closed the lights, closed my eyes

to his lean arms—his father's arms
locked in cuffs, folded down

into the police car, eyes straight ahead
a man, my son, a man.

The fourth night, the fifth night I said nothing
kept it in my mouth, kept it in

my skull, the tentacled fear reaching down
choking out the air. There is so little air

for mothers without sons without money.
Hammers to a shell, hammers to my spine

the newspapers, haole women who float above—
what are they; roots to a lie, what are they; ladders to hell.

I sweep the porch slow
as the week passes, as the radio jabbers

as the walls get closer there is still enough room
in the day to boil potatoes, hang clothes on the line, room in the day

to visit my son to ask him
what all mothers ask, what all helpless mothers

ask "Do you have enough to eat?" The truth:
each night is a stone, each day bitter water.

At the bus stop, I light a cigarette with nothing left to do
but wait.

—Christy Passion

Waiting for the Newspapers

In 1931, the *Hawaii Hochi* and the *Nippu Jiji*
had many readers and included sections in English
for Japanese who were second generation in Hawai'i.

"You wen read da *Hochi*? Dey came up wit some good questions."

"No make sense, yeah. How come had plenny witness who saw
all da suspects far away from da crime scene when da rape happen?"

"No make sense. No mo evidence dat da lady was in dea car,
and her dress stay in good condition."

"Funny kine. Even had one haole guy walking behind her da time of da rape."

"Dey no mo any odda suspects? Cuz sound like dese guys neva do nothing."

Advertiser editorials claimed that Hawai'i was unsafe for women.
Both the *Advertiser* and the *Star-Bulletin* published articles
that assumed all suspects were guilty.

Thalia's name was missing
from the *Advertiser* and *Star-Bulletin* for months,
but photos with names and addresses
of all suspects were included in the papers.

Although the trial did not start,
there already was a difference
in what people in Hawai'i thought of this case
based on race.

—Ann Inoshita

Based on Race

Once, long ago,
my neighbor friend said:
We, the under-dogs.
We don't have a chance.
Look the Fukunaga boy—
in no time, they hang him.

Remembering this,
my heart gave way in anguish
when they took my son away,
the middle of the night.
　　Accused.

I didn't want to show my face.
So ashamed,
I didn't want to go out
of my small home in Hell's Half Acre;
scared too, for I saw everything
in our outside world
as too big.
　　White.

For I had forgotten...
we breathe like them,
eat like them,
dream like them.
The only difference?
We, a different color.
　　Not white.

Once, I had big dreams.
I thought, perhaps,
my children would someday
break the land covenants,
go to college.
I broke my back, my fingers,
to raise my children right.
Even forgot those in Japan,
my family's history beginning here,
and now, turned
    Nightmare.

My Horace is in jail
with the other boys,
accused, not only by the white woman
but by my eyes of shame.
What did the mothers do wrong?
I have to keep reminding myself—
    Nothing!

Our boys? They're good men—
but now they rot in jail.
Put there, without charges.

—Juliet S. Kono

Without Charges

They wait in jail, these no names
crushing knuckles against the concrete wall
wondering how it happened.

In her house in Mānoa
Thalia Fortescue Massie
engraves her father's name, Granville,
into his cousin's name,
Theodore Roosevelt.
Then she melds her grandfather's cousin's name,
Alexander Graham Bell,
into the armor of her story.

Her allies amass their titles and weight:
Rear Admiral Yates Stirling, Jr., Commandant of the U.S. Navy,
enlists his friend, Walter F. Dillingham, Baron of Hawai'i Industry.

In response a counterbalance develops.
A mother calls a princess, Abigail Kawananakoa, who calls a heavyweight:
William H. Heen, born of Hawaiian and Chinese parents,
educated at Hastings Law School, first non-haole judge appointed
to the First Circuit Court (since resigned), leader of the Democratic Party.

To his team he adds a crackerjack haole lawyer from Vicksburg, Mississippi:
William Buckner Pittman, descendant of Francis Scott Key. With the Star-
Spangled Banner on this side, Robert Murakami, graduate of University of Chicago
Law School, joins to even out the battle.

—Jean Yamasaki Toyama

Joins the Battle

Setting: 1

Above him, in a large black and white photo, a battleship churns forward through white foam. The photo is stationed in a curved silver embellished frame. One of the few curved things on stage. Most—the desk, leather chair, pressed uniform, and clock—have an elegant yet Spartan quality: straight, angular, hollow but sharp. Like the sounds of sailors' footsteps against metal ladders.

The smells, the sounds, all is gray.

In relief your attention is drawn to features that contrast: a large gold ring on his right middle finger emblazoned with a star, determined blue eyes, and silver hair at his temples. An open pack of Lucky Strikes lies on the desk near a picture of him shaking hands with Hoover. He is squared off with the president. His face is open, jaw chiseled: Hollywood.

The admiral is at his desk studying strategic plans or he is at the bookshelf reading a week-old *New York Post*, or he is sitting just off to the side of the room journaling private thoughts while sipping bourbon.

The phone rings twice before he picks it up. The voice on the other end is nervous, twitchy, "Sir, one of the officers' wives was raped last night. A submariner, Massie."

Imagine: 2

(*Spotlight on the admiral, everything else fades to black.*)

He stands, a bent mountain, knuckles to the desk. His face is troubled.

He looks to the right where light filters through an opaque window, a vision:

yellow lace and white floorboards
young women playing bridge and drinking tea on the porch
slender fingers balancing fragile porcelain cups up to pale puffed lips
He looks over his shoulder to the left; another vision:

her legs are flayed open
the green silk slides over the garter drawn up by brown hands as cold and hard as
the moon
her breath comes in short staccato pink petals—bruised and wet
knees lock to the inside of hers as a breath is pushed an inch away from her mound
of wiry black hair
their breaths in unison now, deafening
her neck stiffens

He closes his eyes, face down.

A dog is heard howling outside the window.

Gunslinger: 3

(Lights up.)

The admiral kicks the door to his office open, slamming it to the wall,
knocking the picture of Hoover to the floor as the battleship tilts to a
downward dive.

"Get me to the governor." He has the language of ordering, the tone of gutting a pig.

A 1931 2-door navy blue Ford with an American flag streaming from the back
cab pulls up. We see his face as he lowers to get in: his eyes are bright, lips sealed
together.

Admiral Yates steps out in front of the governor's office, 'Iolani Palace. (The theme song from Clint Eastwood's *Fistful of Dollars*, "Titoli" begins to play.) The air is warm and humid. He turns to face the palace. He is wearing a blue work shirt, dusty and streaked, with guns holstered on the crests of his hips. The guns and holster are worn, smooth brown handles and fitted leather.

Evenly, flatly, we hear his last words, "Not in my America."

He takes long strides toward the palace as dust kicks up and obscures the view.

—Christy Passion

Viewpoints

(This scene is at Queen Kapiʻolani Maternity Hospital in October 1931. Doctors and nurses are busy helping patients.)

NURSE 1: Thalia Massie is in that room. *(Points to her room.)*

NURSE 2: What is she in for?

NURSE 1: She had a curettage.

NURSE 2: Curettage?

NURSE 1: Yes, but the results were negative. She's not pregnant.

(Nurse 2 looks at Nurse 1.)

NURSE 1: I know. Other nurses also wonder about the rape.

(Grace Fortescue enters to visit Thalia. She stares at the two nurses and is upset. She immediately finds the administrator.)

GRACE: *(Stares at the administrator with disapproval.)* I want only white nurses to be with my daughter. No niggers.

(The administrator is puzzled and looks at the Asian and Hawaiian nurses. Then looks back at Grace.)

GRACE: *(Repeats her request impatiently.)* Am I not clear? Only white nurses. *(Grace enters Thalia's room and continues to complain.)* Thalia, I can't believe this place! Even where we live, there are niggers who have been living in Manoa for generations! Holding their luaus...I can't believe they're allowed to live in our neighborhood. *(She sighs.)* Thank God, the military now has many who have strong values like we do.

(The two nurses and administrator stare at Thalia's room, puzzled. Then another patient enters the hospital. Nurses, doctors, and staff continue with their work.)

—Ann Inoshita

Of Strong Values

the Buddha says
there are three poisons in life:
greed, anger, ignorance.

   of *greed*
where the white man once came
and sucked everything dry
the ahupua'a
one's breath
one's body
one's heart
the kaiaulu winds

takes many forms
their religion's
need to convert
with great speed
the Noble Savage
lest the natives
be condemned
to hell

   of *anger*
at the violation
of one of their women
pure and white
in the fairy tale
of their one-mind's eye

oh it's okay
if they beat and kill

their own women
but don't let anyone else
touch her
especially the outsider
the locals
oh no

later they will take it upon
themselves to beat up the Jap
and scheme to kill
the darkest of them all

    of *ignorance*
when Stanley Porteus
implies whites
are superior to other races
therefore other races
are expendable
when he later has a building
named after him
at the University of Hawai'i
that's ignorance

when people believe
that theirs is the one
and only true god
that's ignorance

when people think that they
have all the answers
and that their shit don't stink
that's ignorance

—Juliet S. Kono

That's Ignorance

That's ignorance for you!
We've been at it since December 2nd. Gone over
all the testimony, hashed out all the details,
and you still can't come to a verdict.
How many times are we going to vote? 100?
Seven to five for acquittal.
Seven to five for conviction.
Hey, we can't have it both ways.

Come on, for me it's clear. Guilty!
I don't want to be here until Christmas.

OK. OK. Go over one more time. The problems.
For one thing, her testimony different from the first report.
Then, the timing. No can happen.
And one more thing, the police. Who to believe?

Hey, she saw her attackers clearly.
She remembered some nicknames.
She saw the license plate number. What more do we need?

Yeah, yeah. First she said she couldn't see.
And she said, all Hawaiian. She remembered the name, "Bull."
Nobody named "Bull." She said was after midnight when she wen leave the dance.

She correct herself, that's all. When she calm down, she
say 11:35. That work!

Works? Are you kidding? Kidnapping,
driving, 4-6 rapes, in 20 minutes?

No can...

Sure can, the prosecutor show how.

What about the tire tracks? Officer Benton
said they matched the Ida car perfectly.
Yeah but, he said he saw them 4 hours after the attack
but it was really 30 hours afterwards. And Officer Lau,
he refused to take a picture. Maybe those marks were put there
later.

What! are you saying the police are corrupt? Bastard!

Hey! No fight...

If only walls could talk.

—Jean Yamasaki Toyama

If the Walls Could Talk

Dearest Margaret,

I so envy you—

Downtown must be ablaze with Christmas decorations and everyone
would have their invitation to Amanda's party by now—I shall miss it all!
The laughter, the clinking of glasses, the Colonel's nephew and his glorious lips—

I shall miss your entrance, luminous in the latest from Paris;
I would be there with you, we a pair of doves—no, not doves, moonlight
spilling onto everything—onto the flowers, the baskets of gifts,
the lapels of men—no one can deny the moonlight.

Every detail of the last soiree we attended together is still fresh in my mind
Oh if the walls could talk! Collapsing and crumbling into a hail of champagne,
rivers of it running through and around us. I see the rainbow lights

from the grand hall chandelier reflecting like gems in your curls. There is no
such light here. It's pale blue and sticky heat, palm trees and dirt roads,
a changeless old that builds up from the ground and waits.

It buzzes and swells in the wrong-skinned people here,
I see its disapproval in their eyes. I want to be free of it, run from this place,
fly over the trial and mother and Tommie—way beyond this eternal summer

harnessing me here. Yes. I do know that summers eventually eclipse
turn to autumn with its brilliant reds and orange fires.
Fires that can burn it to the ground, burn it clean.

Lord knows it's not autumn, Margaret,
and even with the sun blaring

I can't seem to forget
this winter has just begun.

Thalia

—Christy Passion

Winter Has Begun

My poor daughter. It outrages me to no end
how the court system could free savage natives
with their filthy mixed breed origins
with no conscience and no godly respect for the white race.

A mistrial. My heart can't believe this.
A mistrial purely based on the cunning ways of the defense
with no thought of vindication for my Thalia.

This trial should have been the end
to all whispering, dirty talk
about my daughter, my bloodline.

Judge Steadman was of no use to me.
Steadman didn't jail the natives.
Instead, they were out on bail.

Stirling was of no use to me either.
Stirling asked the acting governor, Brown,
to toss the savages in jail, but Brown declined.

How could Steadman and Brown
fellow white brethren
turn their backs and not honor their daughters?

Their military brothers have taken action
physically honoring their white sisters
by forcing their fists onto brown and yellow skin.

True Americans would have taken action.
Americans would not have hesitated to grab the nearest rope

and place it around the necks of lesser beasts
to protect their pedigree.

Tommie is at sea, but Deacon Jones is here.
Deacon is dutiful and forthright.
Earlier, he took the Ida boy
and tried to force him to confess.

Although Tommie left a gun for Thalia, I doubt that it's enough.
Deacon, Helene, and I bought guns as well.

I, Grace Fortescue, will never let savages triumph.

—Ann Inoshita

Savages Triumph

How long the trial felt. Seemed years.
Watching the trial was like
watching the leaves of the kamani
trees do their slow twist in the wind,
the sun illuminating
the undersides, as if in a gathering of hope.
They would not be blown away.

To fill the long hours,
I crocheted mechanically,
and winced at the words:
rape, suspects, broken jaw,
an open but clean vagina.

I remember when my son once
brought me a plant on Arbor Day.
The leaves were young, deepening
in green, and I thought him good and kind,
my mother-soul trying to find evidence
of the meanness they accuse him of.

My Joe, did you really hit Mrs. Peeples?
My Joe, did you really rape Thalia Massie?
My Joe, in your goodness, did you really bring me a plant
that spread its branches
in translucent green sunbeams?

Were you capable of all this?

The green of a plant is a hopeful color.
What makes a rapist? Not the vegetation

around the boys who were purported
to have done the deed, the rustle
of the leaves and branches around them,
the breaking of twigs when
a woman was thrown from the car.
There is no evidence of any of this dirt
on her clothes or shoes.

I drop my wooden crochet needle.
It hits the floor with a dull *clack*
through the November that is here,
in the sticky humid winds of our winter.
It's still hurricane weather,
and the jury is finally sequestered.

I read the Bible and the newspapers.
The white people
in the gallery don't believe
I had been educated in the King's English,
and am highly literate,
but they continue to look down on me.
I can feel their eyes
and their hand-me-down hours
like everything I own.
Second-hand, not green and new.

Hung, they finally say:
Impossible to be in two places
at the same time,
the timeline wrong,
a lack of motive,
inconclusive evidence.

And it brings something else
into the surrounding air—
an emergent green feeling,
gratitude to a handful of brave good men,
a greening of the "savages"
the Japanese, Chinese, Portuguese, Filipinos,
and us, the natives, as we
begin to all come together.

—Juliet S. Kono

Come Together

Jeez, their voices hurt my ears
my head is spinning
this floor is cold.
What they saying?

"...come together...in this together..."

"...do justice..."

"...jury wrong..."

"Confess, confess."

Auwe...what she talking
that Fortescue lady
so loud
they push me in the car
drag me here
I can't move

"...we're in this together..."

"...newspapers said..."

"...stop this chaos..."

"...lust-mad youths...
foul, slimy creatures...
attacking the innocent..."

"...forty rapes last year..."

"...martial law..."

What they talking?
Why they shoot me?

"Stay awake, Joey, stay awake?
Joseph! Don't go to sleep."

I hear you, Mommy,
I hear you
It's so hard

I don't want to die...

—Jean Yamasaki Toyama

To Die

You are not here.

Not your smooth skin taut over bones, over warm blood
coursing through your heart.
Heart of a brown mother, heart of a brown father
heart that never confessed
I didn't do anything wrong Daddy, I swear

Not your eyes wide that took in boxing matches and light of a girl's face
not your fingers pulling through soft curls
not your long-legged stride
not your shy laugh that lifted above this crooked path.
Above the unease.
Not the bright memories that kept you whole:
high school dance, cousin's wedding, favorite black comb.
Not even the dark ones: haoles with rope.

And we who are here

do what we must: close the casket,
open the ground, return what was never ours and wonder—
can we take you once more, just once more,
to the places you loved? Go back—
carry you out of this field
bring your lei, your music

take you down to Akepo Lane
past the pool hall's soft thud of a cushioned tip hitting the cue.
Take you to Kauluwela
lean bodies gripping the dirt with toes—feet running, lunging, running.
Drive you along School Street—through A'ala Park

past weathered old Filipinos shooting dice
"Boy, Boy, come!"

Can we take you to the beginning?
back to the cradle when you were a babe
and could only look up; fat and drowsy
imagine not this world for us.
Imagine amazement,
slopes of green, bronze stars in the fishermen's net,
crack lightning in your tongue and veins—
all these within you pushing forward a reckless promise
that is inherent in every creation, Godlike. We.
Maybe there you can rise and let loose
the shame and fear inscribed in our palms

—Christy Passion

No Shame for Murder in 1932

What did Judd expect would happen?
Didn't he know that God-fearing men
protect their women when justice is not granted?

Judd is not fit to serve as governor.
I, Admiral Stirling, marched to 'Iolani Palace to explain to him
that mongrels accused of raping poor Thalia
must be protected in jail cells for their own good.
Otherwise, they may share the same fate as Kahahawai.

Did Judd believe there wouldn't be retribution?
No one could blame
a husband
a mother
and Navy brethren
who sought justice on their own terms.

How dare anyone attempt to jail these good white people?
Judge Christy allowed the Navy to have custody of our guests
aboard the USS *Alton* where they are protected and sheltered
with all the lodging and amenities they deserve.
They are blessed with flowers and messages inscribed with good wishes.

—Ann Inoshita

We Are Blessed

with flowers and messages inscribed with good wishes,
and I think to myself what I really want to say to you
with captured words that never leave my imprisoned tongue.
Thalia, people across the nation agree I did
the right thing no matter what *you* believe.

We wait in this boat, as the government decides what to do with us,
its berths no different from jail cells, except for the privacy.
All day, every day, what are you sniveling about?
My whore wife, child, the whiff of you sickens me,
for you who are nothing but a fucking witch bitch,
who instigated with your cry of rape what we are enmeshed in,
which is not like the pranks we played in Patchogue.
This is real! And you pushed me to anger, like someone
pushes a kid from behind to do something he doesn't want to do.
Thus, I had to go through that dark tunnel and at its end,
fall off the cliff. During this whole time, I had to wonder
who you were—what hemlocks had you walked under,
what lilac branches had you snapped for your bouquets?
Under what sky, what waterfall?—especially when you actually
sully the very leaves you touch, the ground you walk on.
Thalia, Thalia, you dirty everything.

I often wondered about us, the forces that drove us—
your liquor, your mother, my honor—the unremitting anger
beneath my breastbone that swung like a pendulous knife
above our lives. Once set in motion, there was no turning back.

Lovely daughter, my once lovely wife.

No one knows better than I,
as to who or what you really are,
though I must admit you put on a good show,
walking with your head on a pike, looking hurt but avenged,
lifting eyes full of pride, crying with your handkerchief
up to your nose as if you are breathing in the fresh
scent of the white rose you hold. That's during the day,
in the light. But at night you're a different animal.
You don't touch me, save for the wine glass you suck
more tenderly than my manhood. How people would laugh
if they only knew. Whore/wife, I had to do what I did, don't you see?
How could I have done otherwise? Still hold my head high
among white people, like one must hold his head above water
to stay alive? Or die from shame? I could never be bested
by these savages, these niggers, who swam with you and slid
up and down your back on their surfboards, taking the waves to shore.
They could never be above or equal to us. So why
do you mourn what I did in your nightly pleadings?
Why? you ask, *why?* I did it for you, Thalia, for you!
You think I went too far. You hate me for it, don't you?
I can see it in your eyes.

—Juliet S. Kono

I Can See It in Their Eyes

Even in this grainy wedding picture
on the front page.
Look, Harry,
Aren't they so full of love?
Reminds me of when we were married.

What a shame! How can he look at her in the same way
now after the rape?

The News calls it "Honor Killing,"
they felt they had to do it.
My brother says the *Louisville Herald* is carrying the story too.
Must be all over the country, maybe all over the world.

Are you listening, Harry?

Look, here's another picture,
that rapist, Horace Ida.
Look at those slant eyes.
Says here all the trouble in Hawai'i is a Jap plot .

There sure were a lot of Japs in Hawai'i
when we were there on vacation.
Remember? Strange eyes.

My brother says there's a danger of them being tried
by a jury of yellow men for the killing of a yellow man.
That's not right. Doesn't the Constitution say a jury of
equals?

Looks like there's race wars in Hawai'i,
Not a place for decent people.

No wonder they're asking President Hoover to
declare martial law.

You could say that's the end of paradise.

—Jean Yamasaki Toyama

You Could Say

(Deacon's lament)

You could say
it was a long time coming.
Not like a reckoning, not like how
your mother preached at you
'bout the thunderstorms coming
after she caught you behind the shed
fucking the neighbor girl
bare ass in the air
but more like,
a wakening,
a moment that the roads lead to,
and you know it, know it
in your belly that something
necessary is going to happen.

I wanted to tell Tommie *Don't be afraid*
but the day was just too damn hot,
the heat was swollen in my mouth.
Tommie was a boy of books and words
and words and empty hands.
That nigger was no fool,
I paid attention to his wide nose
and the line of his jaw, was ready when
his eyes turned angry. *Tommie,*
words ain't gonna work on this.

Even after Tommie left
the air stayed thick, refusing to rise
what can you do about it?
Shit needed attention

the bathroom floor needed mopping
and spots of blood where the good carpet
used to be, was shouting his name.
My stomach growled
so I tossed back a few more,
I remember thinking you can swallow
fear as much as you can swallow good
and they mostly go down the same.

I push the bloody towels to the side
and find the bullet shell, shove it deep
in my pocket, necessary, when the phone rings;
the cops are coming

It's all come down to this.

—Christy Passion

It's All Come to This

Let's face it, the money's good,
and I wanted to travel to Hawai'i.
I can't believe my life's work has come to this—
I need to sit down.

I wanted to retire when I was fifty,
but I kept working due to disappointing investments.
All those trials:
Leopold and Loeb,
Scopes,
Sweet.
Finally, at seventy-one,
I had enough money to retire.

Then, the '29 crash hit.
How could I have prepared?
My son is in debt; I lost a lot.

Luckily, people know my name, and it helps.
Working with Universal Pictures
and participating in public arguments on religion
brought in money—
for a while.
Now people rather spend their money on the talkies.

All my years of fighting for the rights of blacks—
to have it come to this:
I received a cable with the prospect of defending
Mrs. Grace Fortescue and three men
who killed a native Hawaiian man.
They're paying a good price for my services.

Barnes can't believe I'm here.
My wife says I can do good work in Hawai'i
and help everyone get along,
but I know she doesn't feel right about any of this.

I know what some people are thinking, and I don't blame them.
How could Clarence Darrow be attorney for the defense?

—Ann Inoshita

How Could Clarence Darrow?

Because the law gave him an ethical basis to hide behind money—
defend the indefensible, assail the unassailable—he could.

It is April. The day is warm on the day of the trial, the smell
of coffee fills the halls and for the exhilaration this brings—he could.

To save a son staggering in debt, for his own comfort,
to indulge his wife's extravagances, to pamper his lover—he could.

Notwithstanding being the champion of Blacks,
hero of the Scopes trial and Sweet case—he could.

For the same reasons he was defense attorney
for Leopold and Loeb, even for attorneys caught bribing jurors—he could.

While a hero of the downtrodden, he infamously defended the owners
who had locked 29 of 30 exits of the Iroquois Theater fire. 506 died.

A chameleon, forever opportunistic, he changed like the seasons,
or the hands of a clock. A master of camouflage, he could change

from the righteous, the rod and staff, to the reproachable,
fire and brimstone, or like the brown praying mantis, into a leaf,

to catch its prey for the *green* he loved best.

—Juliet S. Kono

The Green He Loved Best

The green he loved best was the velvety
color of that drink he had. Where was it anyway—
China? Australia? Fiji?—the one with
the name he couldn't pronounce. "The green one,
you know," he'd say to the bartender.
Not like any drink he had with his brother in Butte,
to wash away copper dust from those Montana mines.

But now in Hawai'i it was not time for a binge
not for John Kelley, prosecutor, not now.
Now was the time for butt-off work.

After all, he'll have a faceoff with Darrow,
that expert of the sleight of hand,
with 30 years experience over him.
He knew he was up against the magician,
who would probably call in alienists to argue the
"alarm clock" insanity—it's only temporary—as a defense.
Or he'll pull the empathy cord. What would you do
in their place? You'd have to defend her honor.

Kelley knows that any trial is over when jury selection is complete.
Could a white jury convict? he wonders.

Then he thinks of the "powder room" with lounge and separate entry
they built for Mrs. Fortescue because, of course, she couldn't use the same
toilet as the hoi polloi.

This makes him thirst. He'll need a flood of drink after the trial,
one that would flush it all away.

—Jean Yamasaki Toyama

Gave It All Away

She wore a white kīkepa to the stand
quiet when the prosecution found it necessary to ask
Objection, objection! came from the defense
but the judge nodded for her to reply

The prosecution found it necessary to ask
how many children she had
The judge nodded for her to reply
and no one in the courtroom moved

How many children did she have?
Two children, Joseph and Lillian
No one in the courtroom breathed
listening as she gave it all away

She remembered two children, Joseph and Lillian
But is Joseph alive? A mother's cry
the tremble in her voice gave it all away
The jurors strained to hear

No, Joseph is not alive. A mother confronts
the bloodstained shirt on display
while the jurors strain to hear how
she mended it the night before

Joseph's bloodstained shirt on display
her hands instinctively reach out to it,
she sees the mending from the night before
proof that she took care of her son

She instinctively reaches out to him
lets the tears fall as the prosecution rests
proves she is still taking care of her son
enduring in her white kīkepa to the stand

—Christy Passion

To the Stand

Clarence Darrow called Thomas Massie to the stand
to show how his wife's assault and related events thereafter
affected his mental state and resulted in Kahahawai's death.

Psychiatric authorities testified, and Thalia testified
on how her circumstances affected Tommie.

Darrow pondered during his closing argument:
What would anyone do in this situation?
What if you were the husband or mother of Thalia?

For the prosecution, John Kelley's closing argument was simple:
A man was murdered.
What if you were the mother of Joseph Kahahawai?

—Ann Inoshita

What If You Were the Mother?

Of Joseph Kahahawai

I would grieve all my life.
Though the grieving would change over the years,
the angry shark of it that attacked my gut,
lessening its hold on me in time.

But I can guarantee you one thing.
Every morning when I wake up,
something of it would be back at my doorstep
like the old familiar neighborhood stray cat
let in to curl at my side for the rest of the day.

And this grief would well up
at odd moments in my life.
When I see the face of a child at the window
looking out, or a boy on his bike,
cards between the spokes,
making sounds in the wind.

Or, at a sudden rain, splattering
its droplets
upon the roof of my memory.

It would serve as a memento—
the stone I carry in my pocket,
the golden locket I hang around my neck.

This grief would rise up in me
when I see a rainbow or the setting sun,
or when I smell his shirt still hanging

in the closet and, once in a while, take
up to my face. Be overcome
by his scent. I would drop to my knees
and fall to the floor and slap
the hard dark wood with my hands
while I would scold myself: "Don't do this!"
I will never stop.

I wouldn't be able to help myself,
grief the only way to be closest to him.

Of Thalia Massie

Looking back at this mess,
as an old woman,
I can tell you that my pain and
suffering never ceased.
Who is to know another's suffering?
For retribution comes one way
or another. I learned this
too late,
despite my triumphant release,
the commutation, the one-hour sentence
I spent drinking champagne.
In triumph? Perhaps. In the end, however,
I endured a greater sentence—
a life sentence of regret and remorse.
Never for killing Kahahawai, however.
I still have a cold heart where he's concerned
for I believe he was the perpetrator.
But for the pain I felt for my daughter
as I watched her plummet
as if from the cliffs of the Pali,

becoming an alcoholic, a drug addict,
and at the end, someone who tried
to commit suicide once, twice,
succeeding on the second try,
her body found in some cheap hotel room.

I have to admit. I shared the same
grief as Joseph Kahahawai's mother,
for wasn't I as passionate a mother
as she had been when Thalia was brutalized?
Wasn't our suffering the reason for Tommie's and my
wanting to murder her son in the first place?

Thalia's suffering, my suffering,
Thalia's pain, my pain,
her death, my death.
I was heartbroken when I went to collect
her body and bury her in the cold
hard ground so far away from your angry
shores where the ripples of outrage
continue throughout the years.

—Juliet S. Kono

Through the Years

we'll forget the dates and details of the alleged rape;

we'll forget the green silk dress, the names of the accused, Tin Can Alley, the make of the car;

we'll forget the who of the defense, the why of the prosecution, the headlines, the dirty accusations, the howling retorts;

we'll forget the hung jury, the cowboy admiral, the kidnap car, the caliber of the gun (what gun?), the mother's smirk (you know which one).

We've forgotten President Hoover who refused to declare martial law and Governor Judd who commuted the ten-year sentence required by law to an hour in his office for the killers to toast their punishment with champagne; but

tell me what must we remember?

—Jean Yamasaki Toyama

Commentary

Christy: A Prelude

I knew nothing about the Massie-Kahahawai case. I remember my father
mentioning the trial from time to time when I was growing up. *Those haoles
murdered that kid and got off with nothing, not one day in jail.* Of course though,
not wanting to take yet another trip down nostalgic 1940s Akepo Lane*—
trips my father never tired of while reliving his glory days—I tuned him out.
I didn't have time for more old stories. Fast-forward to the present, when we
decide to embark on a creative project about one of the most infamous trials
in Hawaii's history. I am much older, learning for the first time about events
that shaped not only the islands but also, closer to home, my father, and as a
result, me. The rich knowledge of my father living in the wake of that ordeal
and the texture of that time were lost to me with his illness and now, his
recent passing.

In the coming months, I'd be horrified, outraged, and would at moments feel a
true sense of loss as I poured myself into learning and writing about this case.
Prior to this newfound knowledge, I was smug in my cultural identity of being
Native Hawaiian. (I'm also part Filipino, Chinese, and Portuguese, and I'm pretty
smug in those identities as well.) With each turn of the page, my arrogance was
eroded by shame. Not shame in the history of what happened, but shame in
knowing I committed a cardinal sin in Hawaiian culture; *my father was trying to
impart knowledge to me, and I didn't listen.* I could just hear my kumu hula *tsking* and
nodding her head in shame.

I could not read David Stannard's book, *Honor Killing*, for more than several pages
at a time. I stopped frequently to curse at the injustices committed and more
directly at those (long dead now) who engineered the offense. I began to reactively
blurt out *fuck you* whenever driving under the Dillingham Boulevard freeway sign.
(Walter Dillingham was a prominent white businessman in Hawai'i who held
racist attitudes against non-whites. He used his influence to attempt to sway the
outcome of the trials in favor of the Massies.)

> I skip to the end where she commits suicide
> and like a child burning ants, feel a false sense of power
> the end gathers me up for the journey back

I did skip to the end of the book. I couldn't take it anymore. I needed to know that justice would prevail. I needed something bad to happen to the people who did really bad things. But for the most part it didn't. Thalia's suicide years later was the closest I would get.

These past violations resonated with me as echoes in my life. There were so many stories my father told me about shady cops, and job opportunities he missed because of his brown skin.

> Chris, no can believe was so hard
> but we work, talk story,
> forget for little while
>
> This is not Michener's Hawai'i

Midway through *Honor Killing* is where it clicks for me, the *aha* moment. The parallels of my father's stories running alongside the bitter truths of that time materialized for me. The prejudices, the loyalty, the weaknesses and strengths in my father's words had a genesis. Here, in this rotten trial, and all the steps that led to it, formed the boundary of my father's beliefs. These passed down to me. It was apparent in that *aha* moment, that starting the first poem of this project would have to introduce the history of this case as well as the fallout which remains in the present.

> This story is the unwanted family heirloom

I realized there was no way we would ever catch all aspects of this faceted case in this project, even though we were naively hopeful that maybe, somehow, perhaps we could. We were not even remotely close. There were important voices we didn't touch (none of the other boys who were accused were attempted), the links pushed along too quickly—so many important events not relayed. It was the most painful story I had to sit with and interpret. But if there was shame in turning a deaf ear to this story earlier when my father tried to teach me, how much more so if I chose to keep quiet about what I had learned? I needed to try.

*Akepo Lane is in one of the poorer districts of Honolulu, Kalihi-Palama, where my father grew up and where several defendants in the trial of the rape of Thalia Massie also lived.

Reading Assignment: Stannard's *Honor Killing*

I don't want to read this story.

Don't want to know their names, imagine their faces.

I catch my breath as the words surface:
Tin Can Alley, bare feet football,
brown-skinned boys wearing white silk shirts.
See them behind the wheel—immortal for the night;
hear the ease in their laughter
stronger than daylight and the poor.

Too close to home.

It is my father's stories of his Hawai'i.
There were few comforts, but
there were dances at the Ala Wai Club,
Violet's in Kalihi—stew bowl for 25 cents,
there were beatings, Japs, Haoles, Blahlaz, and curfew;
dirty cops way too willing, rats that climbed up
tin gutters, girls with nice legs who gave it up
easy, and if you were lucky, real lucky,
a job at the shipyard.

*Was different back den Chris
no can believe, was so hard. But we work,
go drink, talk story, forget for little while*

This is not Michener's Hawai'i.

I skip to the end where she commits suicide—
and like a child burning ants, feel

a false sense of power. The end gathers me up
for the journey back.

This story is the unwanted family heirloom
the ugly vase,
the chipped china,
the bastard child everyone whispers about,
but no one calls by name.

Ann: A Day in History

Before we wrote poems based on the Massie and Kahahawai cases, we all agreed to
read Stannard's book *Honor Killing*. Juliet was already familiar with these cases. I
was assigned Stannard's book as required reading for a graduate class; it was hard
to read the book because I am Japanese, American, born and raised in Hawai'i
(4th generation), and I would have been the object of racism during the 1930s had
I lived then. As a student, I skimmed through the book because I was appalled
by the injustices and hatred toward any non-white person. In the continental
United States, it was the time of lynching and discrimination based on a belief in
a superior race. Years later, I still couldn't stomach it, but I forced myself to read
every sentence, page, chapter, in small portions at a time. Stannard had done his
homework; I looked at the list of research sources for each chapter at the back of his
book. I thought of a past visit to Hamilton Library on the University of Hawai'i at
Mānoa campus. As a student, I remember reading dated sources with white racist
voices denouncing non-whites as inferior. I couldn't handle it. I returned sources
back to their shelves. I wanted to forget. I wanted to unlearn everything that I read.

I do not remember learning about these cases in public school during the 1970s
and 1980s. If I was not ready to learn about the Massie and Kahahawai cases as a
college student, I was certainly not ready to learn about them at a younger age. This
being said, I also believe that history explains the behavior of people today. With
knowledge of the Massie and Kahahawai cases and this poetic historical journey with
Christy, Juliet, and Jean, I have a deeper understanding of why residents in Hawai'i
behave the way they do as a result of past treatment from earlier generations.

After I read Christy's prelude, I realized that I was responsible for the first poem that set our historical journey in motion. My body turned red; my skin was hot. I was perspiring. I felt a responsibility to give the facts and not embellish anything. The facts that I included would haunt the rest of the poems because I would record what happened on Sunday, September 13, 1931. Most of the facts came from Stannard's book. It was important to note that two events were reported that historic morning. The first event was a report by Agnes Peeples. She and her husband were on their way home when they encountered another car with male passengers at an intersection. Both cars evaded an accident, but members from both cars engaged in a heated argument, resulting in Agnes Peeples' report to the police:

> Before the call came, Agnes Peeples
> walked into the building at 12:45 a.m.
> Agnes said her husband was driving
> when they encountered a car filled with men
> where King and Liliha intersect.

The second event was a phone call by Tommie Massie that would lead to Thalia Massie reporting that she was raped:

> The phone rings at 1:47 a.m.,
> so Captain Hans Kashiwabara picks up.
> Tommie Massie reports an assault
> and wants the police to visit his house.

These events are important since the suspects accused of raping Thalia Massie were in Agnes Peeples' report. Therefore, the suspects could not have been in two places at the same time. The last line of the poem "and raped her six or seven times" was given to Juliet, and she continued the poetic journey.

One Call: Sunday, September 13, 1931

> Saturday night wasn't busy in the Kapi'olani building,
> so no one from the Honolulu police could predict
> an early morning phone call
> that changed Hawai'i forever.

Before the call came, Agnes Peeples
walked into the building at 12:45 a.m.
Agnes said her husband was driving
when they encountered a car filled with men
where King and Liliha intersect.

Although the cars didn't hit,
Agnes and a man from the other car fought,
resulting in blood seeping from her ear.
She remembered the car's license number: 58-985,
and Officer Cecil Rickard recorded her statement.

The phone rings at 1:47 a.m.,
so Captain Hans Kashiwabara picks up.
Tommie Massie reports an assault
and wants the police to visit his house.

The captain calls Detective John Jardine.
Then Jardine contacts Rickard
who instructs police to drive to the Massie home.

Detective Harbottle, Detective Furtado, and Officer Simerson
listen as Thalia Massie speaks:

She was at the Ala Wai Inn
and went for a walk at about midnight
when a car with four or five Hawaiians came by.

She was forced into the car and punched.
They drove her to a secluded area,
removed her from the car to the bushes,
and raped her six or seven times.

Juliet: Voice of the Dress

I remember Christy, Ann, Jean, and I, immersing ourselves in the study of the
Massie-Kahahawai case. After our first meeting, Christy's first poem that started
the *renshi* cycle appeared on the Bamboo Ridge Press website two weeks later. I was
blown away!

Contrary to the one-week time frame we allowed ourselves to write each poem in *No Choice but to Follow*, we gave ourselves two weeks to write each linked poem on the Massie-Kahahawai case. After Christy's link came Ann's, which gave a factual account of events reported to the police on the night of the alleged rape: Mrs. Peeples making a walk-in report at the station about being assaulted by a local male after a traffic incident; naval officer Tommie Massie asking the police to investigate the rape and assault of his wife, Thalia. The last line of Ann's poem states that "they," the young men supposedly involved, had "raped her six or seven times." I reconstituted this line to "They Raped Her" and used it as the title of my first poem, which I wrote in the voice of the green dress Thalia Massie had been wearing that night. I used the voice of the green dress because I didn't particularly want my poem to be in Thalia's voice, her story about the rape deeply flawed. I did not feel she could be the speaker of my first poem if I saw her as an unsympathetic character and unreliable narrator. I didn't know how to represent her fairly. This is my rather short explanation as to how and why I came to talk about the rape from the dress's point of view.

Later speculation held that some person—a lover, perhaps, or even Tommie Massie, her husband—or persons other than the men accused, could have beaten her. Furthermore, there were indications that she may not have been raped at all. In fact, there was no physical evidence of sexual activity, though she claimed she took a shower before the hospital examination.

I made several deletions when writing this poem, but will talk only about the most significant. In the beginning of the fourth stanza, I wrote about the *ghost* of this dress having premonitory thoughts about more recent events, such as the Deedy case in 2011 when a Federal Special Agent and a local part-Hawaiian male got into an altercation at a McDonald's in Waikīkī and the local man was shot and killed. I wanted to present the idea that we are still haunted and influenced in our collective psyche by our memories of the Massie-Kahahawai case. People immediately latched on to say, in the newspapers or on TV, that aspects of the 2011 case paralleled the notorious case that occurred in 1931. The circumstances of the Deedy case, however, turned out in reverse. This time, the local male looked as if he were the wrongdoer, instead of the haole from the mainland. After much thought, I deleted this part of the poem. For one, the poem was too long; for another, what I deleted diverged from the Massie case and affected the unity of the poem. Additionally, the deleted lines seemed to take on a different tone. The following is what I removed from the poem while in draft form. The speaker, the "I," is the green dress:

> I am there when the brah
> on the street says:
> *Eh haole, what you looking at?*
> *You like beef?* Or when the local
> male can't understand why he hates
> guys in uniform and feels
> like he wants to punch them out,
> but will sign up
> to fight with them in Iraq
> because he needs a job.
> He does what he does,
> but can hardly wait to bug out.
>
> I'm there when the haole looks
> at a local kid "funny kine," or can't
> look him in the eye because
> he's not white or thinks
> the kid's stupid because
> he can only speak "da kine"
> you know, Pidgin,
> and eyes him up,
> as if he were low class,
> uneducated, poor. Trash.
> Animosity working both ways.

Another fault regarding this section? It was too didactic. This does not mean I was not concerned about the injustice or justice of the Massie-Kahahawai case, which survives, overtly or quietly, in Hawaii's multi-layered, multi-generational, multi-cultural society. Whether we like it or not, the subliminal message implicit in this incident rears its ugly head every so often, calling attention to itself, taunting us: *Look at me, I'm still here.* Several cases over the years have paralleled the Massie-Kahahawai case, and since they do keep bubbling up, I had wished to address something about this issue for my own indulgence and clarification. This did not work in its conceit.

In the end, to unify the point or theme of the poem took precedence. I also took poetic license in saying that the dress was burned when, in actuality, it was presented as evidence in the trial and kept by the court. I made this mistake when I wrote the poem and only became aware of this error in my third, much closer reading of *Honor Killing*. I knew then I had to change the last part of the poem, so I created the inference that the green dress had imagined itself being torn across the bodice when pulled off a clothes hanger and "burned in effigy." Jean had already used "Burned in Effigy" as the title and thrust of her poem, so I had to leave my last line intact. I used the burning as symbolic of the sentiment behind what the green dress stood for. It was possibly the only witness to what really happened the night of the owner's supposed rape.

Like most societies and communities, people's lives in Hawai'i revolve around a series of dichotomies, some exclusive, some inclusive: rich and poor, young and old, innas and outtas (insiders and outsiders), winnas and loozzas (winners and losers), haoles and locals, and so on. Where race is concerned—and partially because of incidents like the Massie case, the Katsu Goto case (Goto was lynched, the perpetrators eventually freed), the Myles Fukunaga case (a mentally-ill Japanese American boy was summarily hung for killing a young white boy), and others in Hawaii's history—an underlying tension exists when the haoles look down on the locals or the locals look down on the haoles. As I had stated in the deleted section, "Animosity working both ways."

Growing up, *I did not understand* the condescension, the "they-always-look-down-on-us-second-class-feeling" I got from the haoles' assessment of the way we dressed or acted. *I did not understand* why my haole teacher said that students in Hawai'i were not smart enough to go to colleges on the mainland. The haoles in town looked down on us, especially when we spoke Pidgin, but, as local poet Diane Hina Kahanu maintains in the title of one of her poems, "Just Cause I Speak Pidgin No Mean I Dumb!"

Many years ago, I lived on Chun-Hoon Lane (which no longer exists), in the Kauluwela district. In the 1960s, it was part of a massive redevelopment project; the area was filled with dilapidated tenements. At the time of the alleged rape in 1931, one of the accused, Ben Ahakuelo, a noted boxer in town, lived with his family on Frog Lane, a block away from where I lived in the 1960s with my *then* husband.

I did not understand why my *then* husband and his family (the family I frequently characterized as a bunch of "Japanese Rednecks") used harsh, epithetic language against the haoles in town. In hindsight, I think they probably didn't fully understand why they felt this way either, but an angst existed. *I did not understand* why they would often say things like "stupid haoles" after encounters with haoles or comment, "I would never send my daughters to Punahou School. Get too many haoles." *I did not understand* why locals gave haoles the finger or confronted them with "Eh, dumb haole, you like beef?" and beat them up for inconsequential reasons. Although my *now* husband, who just happens to be haole, was never beaten in an encounter with a local male or males, he was once "called out" by a confrontational bunch when we were walking in Waikīkī one evening.

This learned behavior in my *then* husband's family stems from the fact that their father had grown up in Ahakuelo's neighborhood when the alleged rape occurred, and a few months later, when the revenge murder of Joseph Kahahawai happened in Mānoa Valley. Like many local men of that generation, my *then* husband's father had learned to be terrified of being accused of rape and imagined being powerless at the hands of the haoles. This sensibility, like any prejudice, was then passed down to his sons. Though the jury for the Massie case was not able to deliver a guilty verdict and ended up a hung jury, locals continued to be distrustful of haoles because of the power they held over local people and what they could do with that power. This feeling was galvanized when Joseph Kahahawai, one of young men who had been accused, was murdered by Thalia Massie's mother, Grace Fortescue, and husband, Tommie Massie. Although they, along with two other accomplices, were later found guilty, the perpetrators ultimately served only one hour after their ten-year sentences were commuted by Governor Lawrence Judd. The "you-can't-trust-the-haole" attitude comes out of this memory.

I did not understand all of this until my *now* husband gave me *Something Terrible Has Happened* by Peter Van Slingerland, *Hawaii Scandal* by Cobey Black, and later,

David E. Stannard's book, *Honor Killing*, to read. A movie based on the scandal and several documentaries were also available. I thus realized that much of the tension we feel every once in a while is due—whether we know it or not or like it or not—to the afterlife of the Massie-Kahahawai case. In this sense, the green dress is the ghost of the case that continues to haunt people in Hawai'i.

They Raped Her

she alleged, six or seven times
in her beautiful green dress.
I was that green dress.

Now,
I am the ghost
of that green dress.
These days,
I float ethereally,
from where the Ala Wai Inn stood,
down to John Ena Road
near Fort DeRussy,
where Mrs. George Goeas,
Alice Araki, and Eugenio Batungbacal
testified they saw me pass by,
which places me
in the area late that night.

I am the ghost of the green dress Thalia
wore when she said she was abducted
by five "Hawaiians"
and brought to a place,
dark, isolated, desolate,
in Ala Moana
known as Beach Road,
where only a few
small fishing boats
creaked in darkness
and dogs whined,
their cries coming from the old
animal quarantine station.

I am the ghost of the dress
that continues to weave in and out
of the psyche of Hawaii's people.
Then again that's another story.

I am the ghost of the green dress,
iridescent as the ocean
when in the limu's green-bloom,
a green that accentuated
the color of her fair skin
her light, soulful eyes,
rose-pink lips,
and fine brown hair.
To have seen her,
you would have been
hard-pressed to say
she was pretty;
but unconventionally
attractive, she was taller
than most women in the islands
and had a kind of lugubrious
chicness made of old money
and deep unhappiness,
as she walked away from the Inn
in an inebriated sway.

In the car
where she said she was raped,
I don't remember
if I was lifted gently from her legs
or shoved up to her waist
with trembling hands
or pressed by desire
against the heaving
want and weight
of desperate men.
I don't remember if they nestled
their need into my neckline
as they drooled into her cleavage,
if indeed, they even did.

After whatever happened,
once at home,
I was taken off
and hung like a scarecrow
in her bedroom.
She called the police
to say she'd been beaten
and raped and the detectives
came to take her statement,
but Detective Bill Furtado
and his partner, George Harbottle,
did not inspect me much,
as I swayed in winds from the valley.

Only later was I scrutinized,
whereupon they found but a tiny blood
spot and bit of soil. Nothing more.
I remained green, was clean.

I don't know when it happened,
this part folded into my imagination.
But some months later, *if ever,*
I was stripped from the hanger,
and stomped on, in anger.
Torn from across the bodice,
I was dragged out,
taken to the backyard,
where I was hung and set on fire.
Burned in effigy.

Jean: Voices of Two U.S. Sailors

I watched with great anticipation as each poet posted her link. This time I was last and I saw what a superb start Christy had given us. I was concerned; I had not ever written any poem constrained by actual events.

Juliet couldn't have given me a better line: "Burned in effigy." What a godsend! I had been reading Cobey Black's *Hawaii Scandal* and David Stannard's *Honor*

Killing. Stannard writes that Admiral Stirling, the top military official in Hawai'i in 1931, thought that the preferred punishment for "these dark-skinned criminals" was "to seize the brutes and string them up on trees." So I started my link with:

> "It ain't in effigy I wanna burn 'em
> but in the flesh, real bones, covered in dark skins...."

I wondered about the experience of these young white men, where they came from, how foreign Hawai'i must have seemed to them in 1931. Perhaps, some of them had seen Clara Bow, the It Girl, in the movie *Hula* in 1927. But that wouldn't have told them anything about Hawai'i; just as today, Hawai'i—except for the air shots—is missing from *Hawaii Five-O*. Sure there were hula girl calendars and brochures about cruises to Hawai'i for the super rich, just as the beaches adorn that television program. But where is Hawai'i? The boys in the military rarely saw it. So they must have been shocked when they went to the beaches.

> My own blood boiled seeing them
> black boys right on top—on top, mind you—
> of white girls.
> Even on surfboards it still ain't right,
> skin on skin.

Although Beth Bailey and David Farber wrote about the Hawai'i of the decade of the 1940s in *The First Strange Place*, they provided me with ideas about the reactions of young men from the mainland of the 1930s confronted with Hawai'i.

> Things ain't right here. Color'ds
> don't know their place.

In the beginning of the incident, racism against Hawai'i had not yet erupted in the newspapers on the mainland, only in the military. The trial had not yet taken place, and the newspapers had not yet fueled the outcry against the five. However, Admiral Stirling made his feelings known, in particular, his feelings about the "orange race," what the Japanese were known as at that time. I read this detail in

Stannard's book and was intrigued that the color "orange" later changed to "yellow." It must have been strange for the military men stationed in Hawai'i during the 1930s to see that most of the people here looked like the ones the United States was arming itself against. (Rumors of war against Japan were rampant, and here were people like me and my relatives living as Americans.)

It must have been very weird for the white military men to feel like they were the minority. Most everyone else in the islands was "color'd."

> Two of them are even from that orange race,
> the one they say we gonna fight one day.

As a high school student in the 1950s I didn't know about the Massie case but I do remember the repeated disappointments when we failed to become a state. When Alaska became the 49th state, we students were appalled. I don't remember racism being a major explanation for this snub. But Cobey Black explains that Hawai'i was so besmirched by the Massie case that many lawmakers remembered the affair and thus believed we could never be American.

> "Read those names.
> Ida, Chang, Kahahawai, Takai, Ahakuelo.
> What are they? Not American."

That's how I ended my poem, but I believe that some of that sentiment still exists today. During the last two elections *birthers* were saying that President Obama was not born in the U.S.; I feel it's not because they thought he was born in Kenya, but because to them in some way Hawai'i is not America.

Burned in Effigy

> "It ain't in effigy I wanna burn 'em
> but in the flesh, real bones, covered in dark skins.
> The papers didn't give her name, jus' said 'a beautiful
> young woman, cultured and of gentle bearing.' For
> sure she was white and raped. We wouldn't stand for

that where I come from."
That's what my buddy said.
Maybe he's right.

My own blood boiled seeing them
black boys right on top—on top, mind you—
of white girls.
Even on surfboards it still ain't right,
skin on skin.
On the beach they're laughin'
strummin' ukuleles, singin', smilin',
oh, yes, smilin'.

And then those colored girls here
don't act polite. You say hello, they look
right through you like you not even there.
At home no girl treated me that way.
This ain't no dreamy Hawai'i,
no joy zone. The movies lie.
Things ain't right here. Color'ds
don't know their place.

We heard the Admiral called them rapists,
sordid people, brutes and hoodlums.
Two of them are even from that orange race,
the one they say we gonna fight one day.

My buddy told me I jus' had no guts because
I didn't wanna go down to the jail to burn 'em.
Then he shoves the paper in my face, "Read those names.
Ida, Chang, Kahahawai, Takai, Ahakuelo.
What are they? Not American."

Christy: Voices of the Mothers

Following the chronology where the last line left off, in "What Are They" I
wanted to present an opposing perspective. The preceding poem gave voice to
John Q. American Sailor looking at Hawai'i from the outside in. I wanted to run a
parallel thread, an insider's voice.

I'll admit the perspective I chose, that of a mother of one of the defendants, was a safe one that I could relate to. Not that I have children, but I readily relate to the poor working class and their outlook. My father was a forklift operator and my mother was a baker who worked 16-hour shifts, six days a week. We had the basics covered, but there was precious little for anything else. For those who have never experienced poverty, from a distance it can have a romantic allure. Maybe the vision of tight family bonds or enduring hardships with a smile is what is conjured for some, but that was never my take on it. Having no money is stressful, it robs you of your dignity, and the uncertainties of tomorrow are filled with teeth compelled to bite. I remember the very lean Christmases and my parents' look of shame in not being able to provide more. I remember thrift stores and hunger, the arguments about which bill was more important (the rent? the electric? kids need new shoes?). I remember my mother losing her job and fearing homelessness. The voice in this poem is one without means or options.

I hesitate to speak to the cop/poverty interface. It is politically charged, biased, and completely my own. But you can't talk about the Massie-Kahahawai case without being political and quite frankly, without offending sensitivities. So here goes.

Our country is experiencing a horrific breakdown in relations between police officers and the communities they serve. The Black Lives Matter movement and the corresponding Blue Lives Matter "response" has shed light on the festering wounds of racism, contempt for both justice/injustice, and an outcry to be heard. I waver on speaking about this matter here as I have no experience on either side, not being an African American or a police officer. My opinion, while standing this safe distance away from it, would be close to meaningless. I can share that my heart aches with the all-too-common news coverage of citizens being gunned down or manhandled with seemingly no provocation. That same heart of mine also recoils at reports of police officers being ambushed and the websites that encourage these attacks.

Growing up poor, I had my own experiences with the Honolulu Police Department. Racism exists by feeding off negative stereotypes, often the same ones connected to poverty: being uneducated, a social misfit, guilty by association.

When you grow up poor, cops are not coming into your neighborhood to check on you; they are coming "for" you or your family member or friend. "*You people*" is how they phrased it when speaking to me and, equally common, "*these fucking people*" when they were speaking to each other. I remember the look, the stance, the words and the implied threats of those officers. It built a wall. It is with a me-against-them mentality that I wrote this piece, a disbelief that anything good could happen without heavy payment.

> The fourth night, the fifth night I said nothing
> kept it my mouth, kept it in
>
> my skull, the tentacled fear reaching down
> choking out the air. There is so little air
>
> for mothers without sons without money.

Money matters. I learned early on the people in Kalihi are "handled" a certain way while people in Kahala are "treated" a certain way. Being poor was a great disadvantage beyond just the financial constraints; it meant my voice was not as audible, and that I was less visible. While it has been years since I have had to live that close to the bone, the memories are hardwired in me. My stomach turns and I feel that split second of paralysis when I see images on TV of forced submissions and those being handcuffed then subsequently beaten.

To combat my apprehension, I think about the good people that made and continue to make a difference. Throughout this story, there were people behind the scenes that affected the outcome. Often these "small" acts were heroic, yet unheralded. One of these lesser-known individuals was Identification Officer Samuel Lau. Despite pressure from his superiors and an attempt to mislead him, he refused to photograph evidence that he suspected was planted to frame the local boys. His act of defiance shows the real stuff of what is to be a man of justice and honor. While I'm sure Officer Lau has passed on, I want to say to him *Thank you*, and for standing up to crooked cops, *Right on, Brada Lau, right on.*

What Are They

I said nothing
the night they came, the first night gone

put away the stew warming on the stove,
closed the lights, closed my eyes

to his lean arms—his father's arms
locked in cuffs, folded down

into the police car, eyes straight ahead
a man, my son, a man.

The fourth night, the fifth night I said nothing
kept it in my mouth, kept it in

my skull, the tentacled fear reaching down
choking out the air. There is so little air

for mothers without sons without money.
Hammers to a shell, hammers to my spine

the newspapers, haole women who float above—
what are they; roots to a lie, what are they; ladders to hell.

I sweep the porch slow
as the week passes, as the radio jabbers

as the walls get closer there is still enough room
in the day to boil potatoes, hang clothes on the line, room in the day

to visit my son to ask him
what all mothers ask, what all helpless mothers

ask "Do you have enough to eat?" The truth:
each night is a stone, each day bitter water.

At the bus stop, I light a cigarette with nothing left to do
but wait.

Ann: Local Perspective

In the 1930s, Hawai'i had various news sources in different languages, including Hawaiian and Japanese newspapers. *The Honolulu Advertiser* and the *Star-Bulletin* were printed in English and had a different point of view compared to sources like the *Hawaii Hochi* and *Nippu Jiji*. It is important to include this information since people had different opinions on the Massie case depending on which news source they counted on for information. As a result, many whites had a different opinion of this case than most non-whites. As history has reported this event, we learn that all the defendants were innocent.

As I read Stannard's book, I am reminded that it is important to acknowledge personal bias in order to view facts without prejudice. As I write this commentary, it is the summer of 2016 with a general election for the next president of the United States coming up in November. Currently, there are strong emotions regarding race and immigration and a debate on what America should be. News sources interpret events differently. The source selected for news usually depends on whether a person is a Democrat, Republican, or someone looking for some form of change. Again, opinions are formed and fueled based on which news source is referenced. Again, it is a dangerous time.

The dialogue in this poem is in the Pidgin language. Immigrants from many countries came to Hawai'i to work on the plantations and, in order to communicate effectively, people spoke in Pidgin. Recently, the United States Census Bureau acknowledged that Pidgin is a language. It has variations depending on the time and specific place where a person lived in Hawai'i. When people here speak, it is common to code-switch between English and Pidgin, depending on the situation. In this poem, the word "haole" refers to a white person.

Waiting for the Newspapers

In 1931, the *Hawaii Hochi* and the *Nippu Jiji*
had many readers and included sections in English
for Japanese who were second generation in Hawai'i.

"You wen read da *Hochi*? Dey came up wit some good questions."

"No make sense, yeah. How come had plenny witness who saw
all da suspects far away from da crime scene when da rape happen?"

"No make sense. No mo evidence dat da lady was in dea car,
and her dress stay in good condition."

"Funny kine. Even had one haole guy walking behind her da time of da rape."

"Dey no mo any odda suspects? Cuz sound like dese guys neva do nothing."

Advertiser editorials claimed that Hawai'i was unsafe for women.
Both the *Advertiser* and the *Star-Bulletin* published articles
that assumed all suspects were guilty.

Thalia's name was missing
from the *Advertiser* and *Star-Bulletin* for months,
but photos with names and addresses
of all suspects were included in the papers.

Although the trial did not start,
there already was a difference
in what people in Hawai'i thought of this case
based on race.

Juliet: Voice of Horace Ida's Mother

The car supposedly used in Thalia Massie's alleged rape belonged to Miss Haruyo
Ida, the sister of Horace Ida. As the driver of his sister's car, Horace, though
adamant about not having had anything to do with Thalia Massie's purported rape,
was quickly arrested along with his friends, Ben Ahakuelo, Joseph Kahahawai,
Henry Chang, and David Takai.

Notwithstanding the predicament surrounding the boys, I decided instead to write
a poem from the viewpoint of Mrs. Ida, Horace's mother, because I sympathized
with her plight and felt her anguish, desolation, and isolation. Beyond that, of
course, how terrible it must have also been for the other mothers. Writing this

poem was my attempt to share the other mothers' anxieties in general and Mrs. Ida's in particular.

I wish to touch briefly on Mrs. Ida's background before proceeding. She had come from Japan and had worked as a plantation contract laborer on Maui before moving to Honolulu, where she helped raise five children. When Horace was 21, her husband, Horace's father, a fisherman by trade, drowned in what appeared to be a boating accident. His body was never found. Horace returned to Honolulu from Los Angeles, where he had been living, to attend his father's funeral.

Then, to have this accusation of rape happen to Horace! The anxiety Mrs. Ida felt must have been incredible, an anxiety that came with not being able to eat or sleep. If she did eat, she probably ate her food with tears mixed in, and if she did sleep, it was probably because she was exhausted from crying. It was an anxiety that came from hand-wringing worry that must have been excruciating, dependent upon the fear of something even greater happening because of racial prejudice and her family being poor, things she and her community would have found difficult to control. Because of the established oligarchy, the hope for a good outcome—such as what Mrs. Ida and the other mothers would have been wishing for—was out of their hands.

I begin the poem with the allusion to another case I mentioned earlier, the Myles Fukunaga case, where a mentally-ill Japanese boy had kidnapped and killed a young, white, male student from Punahou School. Mrs. Ida begins by saying:

> Once, long ago,
> My neighbor friend said:
> *We, the under-dogs.*
> *We don't have a chance.*
> *Look the Fukunaga boy—*
> *In no time, they hang him.*

I remember wanting, in the beginning of this poem, to establish the idea there existed a fear of unfairness surrounding Thalia's purported rape. It loomed largely in many local people's minds for it had precedent, that if you were not white, justice was different and swift, which brought me to the Myles Fukunaga case. After Fukunaga had been arrested, Judge Alvah E. Steadman cut the requisite time to observe and assess this young Japanese man's mental condition in half. Later, there was no stay of execution for someone clearly insane, no delay in his punishment. Myles Fukunaga was therefore tried in a matter of days, found guilty, and hung in about a month's time. In the first stanza of the poem, Mrs. Ida's neighbor reminds her of this injustice, its possibility, not to be cruel, necessarily, but to help Mrs. Ida face what could be an inevitable outcome. In other words, the pervading general feeling in the community must have been that the cards were stacked against the young men accused of the crime.

The next part of the poem has Mrs. Ida afraid to show her face because she is ashamed. She is also afraid to leave her home because the outside world seems large and threatening. As she states, *I saw everything/ in our outside world/ as too big / White/.* Through internal dialogue, I then have her stating more of her feelings, and finding that she is no different from the whites in town, the only difference between them, the color of their skins.

> ...we breathe like them,
> eat like them,
> dream like them.
> The only difference?
> We, a different color.
> *Not white.*

She questions: what made the whites in town different from anyone else or so special that they could frown and look down on others like her? However, she also knows the whites in Hawai'i could harm her and her family and friends, control and stifle their wishes and needs by threatening their jobs or increasing their rents. Manipulate and maintain their will on people like her. For weren't they already dictating what happens on the *outside*, in the government and greater community, to people like Mrs. Ida and her friends who were of a different color and race? Although she was as human as they were, there was still a great divide between her and the haole. Because she was not white, the color of privilege, the laws could be different for her and her kind, all because a large part of one group of people, the whites, had deemed themselves superior in the islands, and sometimes, above the law.

I later have her reflecting on how hard she had worked and the aspirations she held for her children. *Once, I had big dreams*, she says, hoping her children would go to college and do something grand, even *break the land covenants*, where only certain groups of people could live in certain areas. She also says she had worked hard to raise her children right, but these dreams had all but dissipated for them and turned into a nightmare because of the crime Horace and his friends had been charged with. And part of her nightmare is because she questions herself as a mother.

Mixed in with her own guilt, Mrs. Ida feels ambivalent about the guilt of her son. Throughout the poem, I tried to portray her anxiety and ambivalence, and though no parent likes to think it, it is also an anxiety conceived of doubt—the *what if*— that crosses the mind of any parent involved in a similar situation. There loomed the question: did he or did he not do this? I truly believe mothers always have these feelings, guilt feelings large or small, simply because we are mothers. We should be able to champion our children, be indomitable in our faith in them, down to believing everything they say, but as everyone knows, this is rarely the case. There is always some doubt. To me, it's an essential part of a mother's nature and inevitable. By the end of the poem, she admonishes herself for thinking Horace had done this horrible deed and rues the fact the boys had been jailed without being charged.

Meanwhile, the temper of the white sentiment in Hawai'i had been directed to the "other." There was a flurry of activity to get these boys, these rapists, and to convict them. There was a lot of race baiting and rumor-mongering in the newspapers, especially from *The Honolulu Advertiser*, which proved to be especially egregious. Under its editor, Raymond Coll, the newspaper was notorious in its vindictiveness and self-righteousness. For example, in an editorial by Coll titled "Something Must be Done," he likened Hawaii's young men to "morons" and described them as "half-baked," saying also that women in Hawai'i were afraid of all the sexual assaults going on (in actuality the numbers were minuscule), the implication being that local men were the culprits in creating this atmosphere. By this time, it was firmly established, mainly through hearsay, that there was a gang rape of a white naval officer's wife by four to five "Hawaiian" boys, although they had consistently denied having anything to do with the woman who said she was raped. Their denials, however, were overshadowed by the machinations of white prejudice that had already been put into place.

Many rumors circulated at this time, many of them eventually solidifying into facts. False conclusions, the coincidence of two assaults—one with Mrs. Peeples in an incident involving her car and Horace Ida's sister's car, and Thalia Massie's alleged rape—occurring close together in time, and perpetrated by the same men, and the highly disputable gathering of solid evidence at the scene of the crime, added to a web of false accusations. As stated before, while even Thalia's rape was highly questionable, and though she was afflicted with very poor eyesight, she still claimed she saw the license plate and could describe the car used in the crime, information she most likely heard announced from a police car. What she told the police took precedence over what the young men in jail said. By this time, the idea of guilt was firmly established. This was what was most frightening to those involved and their families.

In writing this poem, I used a combination of situational history, as in the Myles Fukunaga case and Thalia Massie's alleged rape case, and my ideas concerning the raising of children, of motherhood, and the Japanese culturally based ideas of honor and shame.

This was not an easy poem to write and did not come to me quickly. I began to think perhaps the two-week period to write a poem was more of a handicap rather than beneficial. I dawdled the first week and rushed in the second. Usually, I try to do things right away, but it didn't work for this poem. The pressure was on and I was having concerns; I didn't feel I had a handle on the case itself and felt uneasy writing about it, though one could easily argue that the focus of this poem was not entirely on the case itself, but rather on Mrs. Ida.

Based on Race

Once, long ago,
my neighbor friend said:
We, the under-dogs.
We don't have a chance.
Look the Fukunaga boy—
in no time, they hang him.

Remembering this,
my heart gave way in anguish
when they took my son away,
the middle of the night.
        Accused.

I didn't want to show my face.
So ashamed,
I didn't want to go out
of my small home in Hell's Half Acre;
scared too, for I saw everything
in our outside world
as too big.
        White.

For I had forgotten…
we breathe like them,
eat like them,
dream like them.
The only difference?
We, a different color.
        Not white.

Once, I had big dreams.
I thought, perhaps,
my children would someday
break the land covenants,
go to college.
I broke my back, my fingers,
to raise my children right.
Even forgot those in Japan,
my family's history beginning here,
and now, turned
        Nightmare.

> My Horace is in jail
> with the other boys,
> accused, not only by the white woman
> but by my eyes of shame.
> What did the mothers do wrong?
> I have to keep reminding myself—
>   *Nothing!*
>
> Our boys? They're good men—
> but now they rot in jail.
> Put there, without charges.

Jean: Personal Perspective

Juliet handed me another gift. What other more perfect expression than "without charges" to indicate the inequality of the justice system? People can be jailed without charges. Who gets charged? Who doesn't? Why? Easy answer: money, name, and power. So what I had read about Thalia Massie and her family provided much material for the poem.

It hit me when I read that she lived in Mānoa. I was raised in Mānoa. I knew our family was one of the first Japanese families in our part of Woodlawn, but I didn't know that in the 1930s, 80% of Mānoa was white. That's where the rich and powerful lived. My father always told us that they chose Mānoa because of Manoa School. It took my father, uncles, and their friends every weekend and holiday for over a year to build our house. Ours was a family of carpenters. When I told people I was raised in Mānoa, they thought we were rich.

A place, like a name, evokes all kinds of associations: money, power, status. Thalia Fortescue Massie had a gold-encrusted name, one that gleamed with U.S. power:

> In her house in Mānoa
> Thalia Fortescue Massie
> engraves her father's name, Granville,
> into his cousin's name,
> Theodore Roosevelt.

> Then she melds her grandfather's cousin's name,
> Alexander Graham Bell,
> into the armor of her story.

That's why I used the expression "no name" for the accused to show their lack of power in a society already weighted against them.

> They wait in jail, these no names
> crushing knuckles against the concrete wall
> wondering how it happened.

As for Thalia, her name exudes class with its association with the Greek Muse of comedy, meaning *flourishing*. Thalia herself was not noted for any good humor, though she did engage in pranks. She was related to several famous people, but her father didn't live up to his own name. He was said to be a moocher, living the high life at the expense of others. We'd call them the 1% today.

The names of the U.S. Navy Rear Admiral Yates Stirling, Jr. and Hawai'i industrial magnate Walter F. Dillingham round out this side.

To counterbalance, I found Princess Abigail Kawananakoa, their champion; William H. Heen, born of Hawaiian and Chinese parents; and Robert Murakami. I was happy to see that Japanese name and very happy to see a haole name among the defenders, William Buckner Pittman. His presence reinforced what I had learned as a child: don't judge people by their color or their background, even when it's hard not to.

Without Charges

> They wait in jail, these no names
> crushing knuckles against the concrete wall
> wondering how it happened.

> In her house in Mānoa
> Thalia Fortescue Massie

engraves her father's name, Granville,
into his cousin's name,
Theodore Roosevelt.
Then she melds her grandfather's cousin's name,
Alexander Graham Bell,
into the armor of her story.

Her allies amass their titles and weight:
Rear Admiral Yates Stirling, Jr., Commandant of the U.S. Navy,
enlists his friend Walter F. Dillingham, Baron of Hawai'i Industry.

In response a counterbalance develops.
A mother calls a princess, Abigail Kawananakoa, who calls a heavyweight:
William H. Heen, born of Hawaiian and Chinese parents,
educated at Hastings Law School, first non-haole judge appointed
to the First Circuit Court (since resigned), leader of the Democratic Party.

To his team he adds a crackerjack haole lawyer from Vicksburg, Mississippi:
William Buckner Pittman, descendant of Francis Scott Key. With the Star-
Spangled Banner on this side, Robert Murakami, graduate of University of
Chicago Law School, joins to even out the battle.

Christy: Admiral Stirling's Perspective
(a three-part act in 60 seconds)

Admiral Yates Stirling Jr. is a major player in this event. He was born to a naval
officer and grew up yearning for the adventure his father wrote about in letters to
him during long deployments. His eyes were set on the Navy from a very young
age. He graduated from the Naval Academy in Annapolis and ascended the ranks.
In 1931 he was rear admiral and commandant of the 14th Naval District, which
included Pearl Harbor.

Stirling was arguably a white supremacist. While attending the Naval War College
in Rhode Island in 1912, he wrote an essay entitled "A Military Road Across the
Pacific" arguing the necessity of building military installations across the chain
of the Hawaiian Islands. He viewed Hawai'i as a territory that would be better
controlled by military versus civilian rule.

When reports of Thalia's rape first surfaced, he demanded quick justice to "protect the prestige of whites." He was eager to convict regardless of facts or even in the face of mounting evidence that the accused were innocent. Among his first statements upon hearing about the rape, was *string them up on trees*. His interventions in both the rape and murder trials placed tremendous pressure on the governor by essentially holding Hawaii's economy hostage for his desired outcome of the trials.

I took the easy road with my last poem, by having a voice of someone that I could readily identify with. I knew that I had to move to a different perspective now for the sake of presenting a rounded view (as much as we could anyway). I tried to write in first person, in his voice, but it was horribly contrived. I couldn't suspend myself that far. So the idea came to present it as a play. This way I could show the reader Stirling, as well as have a glimpse into his interior.

Part one is the exterior of the admiral, while part two reveals his mindset, his ideals. I also wanted to place in this stanza, a visual to the rumors that were quickly spreading through the Navy community of what Thalia had gone through.

The final scene, "Gunslinger," brings to life his actions after the phone call reporting the rape of Thalia.

> "Get me to the governor." He has the language of ordering, the tone of gutting a pig.

Stirling orders a staff car to take him to the governor's mansion. Governor Lawrence Judd understood and benefitted from the large sums of money the Navy spent in the islands, as well as the large construction contracts for Pearl Harbor soon to come. After being summoned by Stirling, Judd accepted he had to smooth things over quickly. This acceptance proved to be fatal for Kahahawai.

In the poem I chose a 1931 two-door navy blue Ford for every obvious symbolic reason: 1931, the year of the crime; navy = Navy; and Ford because you can't get more of an American conquering giant in the automotive field than Ford. Not at that time anyway. The scene is clearly meant to evoke an old Western movie feel. I grew up watching Clint Eastwood and John Wayne with my father. This scene is shaded by a sentimental choice to remember that time.

Evenly, flatly, we hear his last words "Not in my America"

I don't think I could sum up the situation coming from Stirling's perspective any more succinctly or precisely than with those four words. Hawai'i was an outsider, something to be kept under control. While in my last poem I reflected on two Americas, one for the haves and the other for the have-nots, this line presents another dichotomy of America, whites versus non-whites.

Joins the Battle

Setting: 1

Above him, in a large black and white photo, a battleship churns forward through white foam. The photo is stationed in a curved silver embellished frame. One of the few curved things on stage. Most—the desk, leather chair, pressed uniform, and clock—have an elegant yet Spartan quality: straight, angular, hollow but sharp. Like the sounds of sailors' footsteps against metal ladders.

The smells, the sounds, all is gray.

In relief your attention is drawn to features that contrast: a large gold ring on his right middle finger emblazoned with a star, determined blue eyes, and silver hair at his temples. An open pack of Lucky Strikes lies on the desk near a picture of him shaking hands with Hoover. He is squared off to the president. His face is open, jaw chiseled: Hollywood.

The admiral is at his desk studying strategic plans or he is at the bookshelf reading a week-old *New York Post*, or he is sitting just off to the side of the room journaling private thoughts while sipping bourbon.

The phone rings twice before he picks it up. The voice on the other end is nervous, twitchy, "Sir, one of the officers' wives was raped last night. A submariner, Massie."

Imagine: 2

(Spotlight on the admiral, everything else fades to black.)

He stands, a bent mountain, knuckles to the desk. His face is troubled.

He looks to the right where light filters through an opaque window, a vision:

yellow lace and white floorboards
young women playing bridge and drinking tea on the porch
slender fingers balancing fragile porcelain cups up to pale puffed lips

He looks over his shoulder to the left; another vision:

her legs are flayed open
the green silk slides over the garter drawn up by brown hands as cold and hard as
the moon
her breath comes in short staccato pink petals—bruised and wet
knees lock to the inside of hers as a breath is pushed an inch away from her
mound of wiry black hair
their breaths in unison now, deafening
her neck stiffens

He closes his eyes, face down.

A dog is heard howling outside the window.

Gunslinger: 3

(Lights up.)

The admiral kicks the door to his office open, slamming it to the wall, knocking
the picture of Hoover to the floor as the battleship tilts to a downward dive.

"Get me to the governor." He has the language of ordering, the tone of gutting
a pig.

A 1931 2-door navy blue Ford with an American flag streaming from the back cab
pulls up. We see his face as he lowers to get in: his eyes are bright, lips sealed
together.

Admiral Yates steps out in front of the governor's office, 'Iolani Palace. (The theme song from Clint Eastwood's *Fistful of Dollars*, "Titoli" begins to play.) The air is warm and humid. He turns to face the palace. He is wearing a blue work shirt, dusty and streaked, with guns holstered on the crests of his hips. The guns and holster are worn, smooth brown handles and fitted leather.

Evenly, flatly, we hear his last words, "Not in my America."

He takes long strides toward the palace as dust kicks up and obscures the view.

Ann: Local Perspective

When we started this project, we agreed that our linked work could take other forms besides poetry. When I saw Christy's three-part act, I was inspired to write a scene with dialogue instead of a poem.

This scene is based on Stannard's research. Since Thalia Massie did not have her menstruation after the reported assault, her mother, Grace Fortescue, scheduled Thalia to have a curettage performed at Queen Kapi'olani Maternity Hospital. They found out that Thalia was not pregnant. Also, nurses at the hospital did not think that Thalia Massie had been raped.

Grace Fortescue did not want an Asian or Hawaiian nurse assisting her daughter, so she requested that only white nurses help her daughter. Fortescue referred to Hawaiians as "niggers." White people arriving in Hawai'i during this time also used this racist word to refer to Hawaiians. Fortescue rented a house in Mānoa, but she was appalled that she lived near a Hawaiian woman's family farm. I included all this information to create the scene. Since this scene is in Grace Fortescue's voice, "Manoa" and "luaus" are intentionally written incorrectly.

I wasn't alive during the 1930s, but I was born and raised in Hawai'i. In Hawai'i, there is a lot of diversity. Although there are biases, stereotypes, and differences in perspective, there is also acceptance and tolerance that we sometimes take for granted. For example, it is not unusual for someone to be Hawaiian, Japanese, Chinese, and Portuguese. Respect for each other is important if you want to fit in. Attitudes and behaviors that represent ideas of superiority or entitlement are generally not accepted in society. In Hawai'i, there is no white majority.

There were many hangings of black people in the continental United States in the 1930s. When I look at history, there is a pattern of actions based on the idea of white superiority and entitlement. Bringing this racist mindset to Hawai'i is strange to non-whites. It's especially shocking since this scene takes place in Queen Kapi'olani Maternity Hospital, a hospital founded by Queen Kapi'olani.

Viewpoints

(This scene is at Queen Kapi'olani Maternity Hospital in October 1931. Doctors and nurses are busy helping patients.)

NURSE 1: Thalia Massie is in that room. *(Points to her room.)*

NURSE 2: What is she in for?

NURSE 1: She had a curettage.

NURSE 2: Curettage?

NURSE 1: Yes, but the results were negative. She's not pregnant.

(Nurse 2 looks at Nurse 1.)

NURSE 1: I know. Other nurses also wonder about the rape.

(Grace Fortescue enters to visit Thalia. She stares at the two nurses and is upset. She immediately finds the administrator.)

GRACE: *(Stares at the administrator with disapproval.)* I want only white nurses to be with my daughter. No niggers.

(The administrator is puzzled and looks at the Asian and Hawaiian nurses. Then looks back at Grace.)

GRACE: (Repeats her request impatiently.) Am I not clear? Only white nurses. (Grace enters Thalia's room and continues to complain.) Thalia, I can't believe this place! Even where we live, there are niggers who have been living in Manoa for generations! Holding their luaus…I can't believe they're allowed to live in our neighborhood. (She sighs.) Thank God, the military now has many who have strong values like we do.

(The two nurses and administrator stare at Thalia's room, puzzled. Then another patient enters the hospital. Nurses, doctors, and staff continue with their work.)

Juliet: Juliet's Voice

When Ann gave me the last line of her play, "Thank God, the military now has many who have strong values like we do," I used the words "strong values" to create my title, "Of Strong Values." Frankly, I did not know what to write about beyond the title. I was in a bind.

After giving it some thought, I realized that the whole Massie case was mixed in with differing values formed by differing groups of people. I agonized over the writing of a poem about values, and while I had ideas as to what I wanted to discuss, I had no clue as to how I was going to put them together. It was soon crunch time, the impulse becoming *use anything in your life to say something.* It quickly became a *do something*—actually, a *write anything*—moment. So I went with the old standard, what all creative writing teachers tell their beginning writers to do: *write what you know!* I do know a little about the Teachings of the Buddha, so I used the idea of the three poisons found in human nature: anger, ignorance, greed, or AIG—yes, like the insurance company—the acronym I use when teaching these three principles to students of the Dharma, The Teachings of Buddha. While we laugh at this acronym, more seriously, these powerful words are important and pertinent points in learning about others and ourselves.

Knowing I don't do well under pressure, I hastily wrote the poem, hoping other ideas would surface and I could revise the poem or write something entirely different before the due date. Of course, I didn't revise or do anything much with the poem once it was written. Perhaps the feeling that I had written something made me not work as hard as I would have done otherwise. Also, real life often gets in the way, and if I recall, this was such a time.

I noticed that this poem took on a different tone compared to what I usually write. It felt more generalized and didactic for one thing, and less imagistic than I would have liked it to be. Gah! I really should have written a new poem because we did have the option to do that, and even at that point in the publishing process, I still had time to write it. But again, this might have changed the ending for Jean's next poem, so I decided to just go with what I had. Daily chores—at work and home—also interfered, and since I had something already written, I went with it. Honestly, at the time, I felt brain dead and without energy to write anything new.

The poem I wrote has a ready-made format of three sections, so that was good. I disassembled the AIG sequence and started with **greed**. In the first stanza I talked about how the white man came and bought up lands and "sucked everything dry" from the Hawaiians. Historically, this was also a time when the Hawaiians were most vulnerable because whole segments of their population had been dying due to the lack of immunity against diseases brought by foreigners. In the next stanza I went on to talk about another form of *greed*, what I felt had been a "religious" greed, the missionaries *zealous* in converting the Hawaiians, the *heathens*, to Christianity. What I wrote in the poem could be thought of as simplistic and open to criticism, but what I wanted to do was bring about a broad-brush sentiment surrounding these ideas, to make people think. Looking back at the poem, I do feel uneasy, because I recognize what I said may have been too simplistic and critically inaccurate as to the missionaries' motivations.

The subsequent three stanzas address the **anger** of white men at the time. In many places across America, there floated the idea that it was okay for white men to beat up, even kill or sexually violate their wives or girlfriends. But it was not okay for anyone outside of that said community to hurt or even look at white women, especially people of color. If someone outside the white community dared touch white women, "they would pay" had been the feeling. Guilty or not. Horace

Ida paid when he was beaten near the Pali and left for dead on the roadside to Kāneʻohe. Joseph Kahahawai paid when he was kidnapped and shot to death. The beating of Ida and the shooting of Kahahawai had been deemed a white man's right, an honorable thing to do. And the others accused of the rape? Their reputations were sullied, and they were stigmatized for many years of their lives, despite being exonerated later on with all charges dropped.

I then moved away from the values associated with greed and in the next three stanzas wrote about **ignorance** found in three very different instances that do not stand together. This is also where I *tell* more than *show* what is going on. What I wanted to do was to highlight and call attention to areas of ignorance readers and people in general need to seriously consider.

Porteus Hall. I passed it every day in the mid-1970s while attending the University of Hawaiʻi. I even remember attending a class there. Only later did I learn about the controversy surrounding the building. Stanley D. Porteus, for whom the building was named, was a former psychology professor at the University of Hawaiʻi. The following excerpt is what I found about him on the Hamilton Library website:

> Stanley Porteus is best known for his cross-cultural research on mental ability. In 1914 he invented the Porteus Maze Test, one of the most widely-used mental tests that does not require either verbal instructions or verbal answers.

> In 1974 the University of Hawaii Board of Regents christened the new political science building Porteus Hall, after noted UH psychologist Stanley D. Porteus. A year later, students and faculty members objected, pointing out that his academic work contained racist and sexist references. The regents reviewed and upheld their decision. [i. e., to keep Porteus's name. (Comment my own.)]

> After a review, the UH administration recommended renaming Porteus Hall in spring 1998, which the board approved. But in doing so, regents asked the administration to review procedures for naming buildings. The building was renamed Saunders Hall in 2001.

What was outrageous about the naming of Porteus Hall in 1974 was that there had been a history of Porteus's way of thinking about the mental abilities of different groups of people, the implication being that certain groups were smarter than others, meaning whites were smarter than any other group. This suggested the superiority of Caucasians over others. How could something like this happen in 1974, after it had been shown conclusively that one racial group was *not* superior to any other? Time and again, theories like Porteus's had been debunked. Those who chose to honor him thus displayed tremendous ignorance. People, understanding the background of this fight, what it meant, wanted to have the name of the building changed, but the decision was upheld by the UH Board of Regents, because of deep ignorance. It took many years of discontent surrounding the building's name before anything was done. The building was finally renamed and changed to Saunders in 2001. Why did it take that long for something that should have been rectified immediately? Discontent in the local community, coming from such insults and memories of them, had been long and abiding in Hawai'i. Locals know how corrosive glorifying someone's legacy that insinuates racism and sexism can be.

I then go on a short riff about ignorance, where people believe that their god is the "one and only true god" and think they have all the answers and believe their "shit don't stink." I wanted to show how this kind of ignorance can be poisonous to the soul, how contemptible it is and corruptible it can be.

Of Strong Values

the Buddha says
there are three poisons in life:
greed, anger, ignorance.

   of greed
where the white man once came
and sucked everything dry
the ahupua'a
one's breath
one's body

one's heart
the kaiaulu winds

takes many forms
their religion's
need to convert
with great speed
the Noble Savage
lest the natives
be condemned
to hell

   of *anger*
at the violation
of one of their women
pure and white
in the fairy tale
of their one-mind's eye

oh it's okay
if they beat and kill
their own women
but don't let anyone else
touch her
especially the outsider
the locals
oh no

later they will take it upon
themselves to beat up the Jap
and scheme to kill
the darkest of them all

   of *ignorance*
when Stanley Porteus
implies whites
are superior to other races
therefore other races
are expendable
when he later has a building
named after him
at the University of Hawai'i
that's ignorance

when people believe
that theirs is the one
and only true god
that's ignorance

when people think that they
have all the answers
and that their shit don't stink
that's ignorance

Jean: Voices of the Jurors

Juliet got us into some philosophy and religion; I wanted to go to the facts, just the facts, to advance the story. The rape trial took place during the month of November 1931, and here we were in December 2011. I can't remember the exact date, but I felt an urgency to get the story of the trial and the jury deliberations into the *renshi*.

I felt like the jurors during the trial, going around in circles. So I turned toward the jury. I remembered Henry Fonda in *12 Angry Men*. Each one of those men saw things through the lens of his own circumstances. One had problems with his son; another wanted to go to a ball game.

Who were these jurors? After two days and many long hours of deliberation, the decision came down to two Chinese, two Japanese, one Portuguese, one haole, and six mixed haole and Hawaiian. According to Stannard—whose book I read religiously—each man had a vulnerable connection, meaning it would be extremely difficult to find the defendants *not* guilty. Unspoken pressure was imposed on them.

I didn't want my link to be a repeat of his book—this was poetry, not history. I wanted to get at the emotion of the moment, like in Fonda's movie. I tried to imply the men's background through their language and give some indication of how they might have felt toward each other. I also wanted to present some of the evidence, some of the actual details of what went on in the voting.

On December 2, 1931, after 8:00 p.m., the jury was told to come to a verdict. Days passed. They couldn't agree. One day a guard heard a chair flung against the wall. Someone shouted, "Bastard." The fight was stopped. The judge lectured them. The jury tried again. In the end, over 100 votes were taken.

It ended in a mistrial.

I had the walls echo the conversations among the jurors; they are talking.

That's Ignorance

That's ignorance for you!
We've been at it since December 2nd. Gone over
all the testimony, hashed out all the details,
and you still can't come to a verdict.
How many times are we going to vote? 100?
Seven to five for acquittal.
Seven to five for conviction.
Hey, we can't have it both ways.

Come on, for me it's clear. Guilty!
I don't want to be here until Christmas.

OK. OK. Go over one more time. The problems.
For one thing, her testimony different from the first report.
Then, the timing. No can happen.
And one more thing, the police. Who to believe?

Hey, she saw her attackers clearly.
She remembered some nicknames.
She saw the license plate number. What more do we need?

Yeah, yeah. First she said she couldn't see.
And she said, all Hawaiian. She remembered the name, "Bull."
Nobody named "Bull." She said was after midnight when she wen leave the dance.

She correct herself, that's all. When she calm down, she
say 11:35. That work!

Works? Are you kidding? Kidnapping,
driving, 4-6 rapes, in 20 minutes?

No can...

Sure can, the prosecutor show how.

What about the tire tracks? Officer Benton
said they matched the Ida car perfectly.
Yeah but, he said he saw them 4 hours after the attack
but it was really 30 hours afterwards. And Officer Lau,
he refused to take a picture. Maybe those marks were put there
later.

What! are you saying the police are corrupt? Bastard!

Hey! No fight...

If only walls could talk.

Christy: Thalia Speaks

Jean's poem propels us into jury deliberations during the trial for Thalia Massie's rape.
It dawns on me after I read her work that the whole reason we are "in deliberations"
now—the voice that fabricated this story which escalated tensions between the Navy
and the locals to a tipping point, the person that was being heralded on the mainland
while at the same time was being met with suspicion here—was not really given any
air time in our links. We talked about Thalia, but we did not give her a voice. While
I could not effectively write from a first person point of view for Admiral Stirling, I
felt more at ease imagining, and thereby speaking, "for" Thalia.

Clearly I am not an aging white military commander hell bent on enforcing "white
prestige," so I hope I am forgiven for kind of copping out when writing about
the Admiral versus writing from his vantage point. I hope, however, that you as a
reader don't conclude that I am comfortable in the skin of an elitist, racist woman
who both actively and passively contributed to the traumatization of strangers. No.

What I could connect to was her loneliness, her desire to go back to how things were. Thalia was overindulged while she was being raised, and taught to belittle people. This upbringing caused her to be a social outcast once she was out of the nest, unable to get along with others, including her husband. Although she was educated she was not bright; school was untenable, a job was unrealistic. There was nothing and no one here for her in Hawai'i. Who among us cannot relate to loneliness? To being the odd man out? To wanting to go back to the time before things turned bad?

The lie that started this mess gave her the attention and "stability" she needed. People rallied around her and her husband stopped, for the moment, asking for a divorce. So while I believe that she needed to keep the façade going to survive, I have to believe that somewhere inside of her, there was also a desire to get off this train, to stop the bright light shining on her story, which she absolutely had to defend. I am trying to hit these notes in a letter I imagine she writes to a friend back home.

In other poems, I place key objects or statements directly related to this event into the work. In this poem, however, there is nothing of historical fact that I include. Somehow I think this is the most truthful poem of the links I penned.

If the Walls Could Talk

Dearest Margaret,

I so envy you—

Downtown must be ablaze with Christmas decorations and everyone
would have their invitation to Amanda's party by now—I shall miss it all!
The laughter, the clinking of glasses, the Colonel's nephew and his glorious lips—

I shall miss your entrance, luminous in the latest from Paris;
I would be there with you, we a pair of doves—no, not doves, moonlight
spilling onto everything—onto the flowers, the baskets of gifts,
the lapels of men—no one can deny the moonlight.

Every detail of the last soiree we attended together is still fresh in my mind
Oh if the walls could talk! Collapsing and crumbling into a hail of champagne,
rivers of it running through and around us. I see the rainbow lights

from the grand hall chandelier reflecting like gems in your curls. There is no
such light here. It's pale blue and sticky heat, palm trees and dirt roads,
a changeless old that builds up from the ground and waits.

It buzzes and swells in the wrong-skinned people here,
I see its disapproval in their eyes. I want to be free of it, run from this place,
fly over the trial and mother and Tommie—way beyond this eternal summer

harnessing me here. Yes. I do know that summers eventually eclipse
turn to autumn with its brilliant reds and orange fires.
Fires that can burn it to the ground, burn it clean.

Lord knows it's not autumn, Margaret,
and even with the sun blaring
I can't seem to forget
this winter has just begun.

Thalia

Ann: Thalia's Mother, Grace, Speaks

After I read Christy's poem written in Thalia's voice, I knew that it made sense to
represent Grace Fortescue's voice in the next poem. My quest was to reveal history
as honestly as I could, and this meant showing Fortescue's point of view truthfully,
without judgment. I went back to Stannard. Grace Fortescue discovered that the
result of the rape case was a mistrial. She had hoped that a guilty verdict would
stop negative talk about her daughter, and she used the words "half-breed natives"
in expressing her outrage. She was a mother who wanted a guilty verdict and
vindication for her daughter, and it was the 1930s when many whites felt that non-
whites should be punished regardless of their guilt or innocence.

Fortescue wanted the defendants to remain in jail, but she was unsuccessful. After
the mistrial, Horace Ida was kidnapped and severely beaten; the group who beat

him wanted a confession, but Ida refused to confess since he didn't rape Thalia Massie. Deacon Jones confessed to Fortescue that he participated in Ida's kidnapping. At the end of the poem, it is revealed that Thalia, Helene (Thalia's sister), Deacon Jones, and Grace Fortescue are now gun owners.

Although I feel that I accurately represented Grace Fortescue, this poem was hard for me to write because I would be the orange/yellow person that she hated. I am not Grace Fortescue. I understand any mother wanting justice and vindication for her daughter, but many whites wanted to punish the accused. It did not matter if the accused committed the crime or not.

Winter Has Begun

My poor daughter. It outrages me to no end
how the court system could free savage natives
with their filthy mixed breed origins
with no conscience and no godly respect for the white race.

A mistrial. My heart can't believe this.
A mistrial purely based on the cunning ways of the defense
with no thought of vindication for my Thalia.

This trial should have been the end
to all whispering, dirty talk
about my daughter, my bloodline.

Judge Steadman was of no use to me.
Steadman didn't jail the natives.
Instead, they were out on bail.

Stirling was of no use to me either.
Stirling asked the acting governor, Brown,
to toss the savages in jail, but Brown declined.

How could Steadman and Brown
fellow white brethren
turn their backs and not honor their daughters?

Their military brothers have taken action
physically honoring their white sisters
by forcing their fists onto brown and yellow skin.

True Americans would have taken action.
Americans would not have hesitated to grab the nearest rope
and place it around the necks of lesser beasts
to protect their pedigree.

Tommie is at sea, but Deacon Jones is here.
Deacon is dutiful and forthright.
Earlier, he took the Ida boy
and tried to force him to confess.

Although Tommie left a gun for Thalia, I doubt that it's enough.
Deacon, Helene, and I bought guns as well.

I, Grace Fortescue, will never let savages triumph.

Juliet: Joseph's Mother, Esther, Speaks

Tense, gripping.

This is how the trial had been for all who were there to observe the proceedings in November 1931. Ann left me with the line "I, Grace Fortescue, will never let savages triumph." I turned the meaning of Ann's last line on its head and named my poem "Savages Triumph." This poem is out of chronological order and should have come before Jean's poem, "That's Ignorance."

Here, I use the voice of Joseph Kahahawai's mother, Esther Anito, to express her feelings as she watches her son being tried for rape. At the beginning I have her crocheting with shaky hands when I didn't even know if she crocheted or not, taking poetic license to show a nervous anxiety that surrounded those on trial and the families involved. (The crocheting image may be an unfortunate allusion to Madame Defarge, who knits during the trials of the aristocratic "enemies of the state" in A Tale of Two Cities by Charles Dickens. Unfortunate, if people do not know who Defarge is and misconstrue the parallel.)

I segue into an imagined old remembrance of Esther's, again not knowing the truth of what I had written about Arbor Day, if it were even part of Esther's and Joseph's experience. This again was something taken from my own experience, where each student was given a small tree to take home, plant, and care for. The idea was to show the softer side of Kahahawai's personality. Books and articles I have read have always characterized him as a gentle person so I wanted to show that side of him. (However, there's the contradictory event with Mrs. Peeples, where she said Kahahawai had hit her across her ear. Later on, this incident turns out to be a large evidence marker, illustrating that the suspects could not have been with Thalia Massie at the time she said she was raped.)

The plants given on Arbor Day were usually Portuguese Pine, which I could never grow beyond a few weeks, the plants usually dying in my care. Throughout the poem, I use the color green of plants, and of feelings generated by the color green, as a metaphor for serenity and balance.

Like Horace Ida's mother, I contend Esther is ambivalent about the role of her son and his friends in the incident. The poem poses a series of questions to show her doubts. At the end, she asks: "Were you capable of all this?" *This* meaning the assault on Mrs. Peeples and the alleged rape, as well as the good things in his nature, such as the plant he brought home to his mother on Arbor Day.

> . . . my mother-soul trying to find evidence
> of the meanness they accuse him of.
>
> My Joe, did you really hit Mrs. Peeples?
> My Joe, did you really rape Thalia Massie?
> My Joe, in your goodness, did you really bring me a plant
> that spread its branches
> in translucent green sunbeams?
>
> Were you capable of all this?

Esther also speaks of how she was looked down upon by the white observers of the trial who were probably thinking she was illiterate and poor, passing judgment on her demeanor, and hoping for a tough verdict because her son and his friends were not white. They would not have thought her schooled in the King's English. Although Hawaiians did not have a written language, once they were exposed to reading and writing by foreigners, they became literate in an incredibly short period of time. By the mid-nineteenth century, the literacy rate for Hawaiians far exceeded that of the whole United States. They had many Hawaiian newspapers, spoke and wrote in Hawaiian, as well as in English.

The poem takes another turn, perhaps premature at this point of discussion, but something I saw already happening, where the local people had been slowly coalescing in their sentiment. I felt that the strong defense lawyers at the trial—William H. Heen, Robert Murakami, and William Pittman—made the case even stronger by hammering Thalia's inconsistent testimony. In the end, the jury could not reach a verdict.

> Hung, they finally say:
> Impossible to be in two places
> at the same time,
> the timeline wrong,
> a lack of motive,
> inconclusive evidence.

I wished again I had more time to revise and work on the poem, but I thought that I did a fairly decent job, considering the exigency of time. While I wanted to scream because I felt this too difficult a subject, not knowing what areas to write about or what to say, I just gritted my teeth and plugged along. We had deadlines to meet.

Because there were so many people involved in what had happened, I looked first at the people involved in the rape trial and then at the murder of Joseph Kahahawai. I began to loosely categorize people involved as "good guys" or "bad guys" when making choices about whom or what to write about. I had already talked about or had gone into the heads of two people I deemed "good guys," Mrs. Ida and Mrs. Esther Anito. Jean had already touched on the "good" lawyers in the rape case, William H. Heen, William Pittman, and Robert Murakami. Ann wrote about the "good" police officers.

Some "good" men I wish I could have talked about were: Judge Albert Christy, who presided over the rape trial; and John Kelley and Barry Urlich, prosecutors of Grace Fortescue et al. in the Kahahawai murder case. To have a juror would have been interesting. Giving voice to a juror would have brought about another dimension to the poetic narration. His presence would have shown that that there were honorable men who believed deeply in truth and justice, and who were on the side of the people. And, of course, from this, I could explore what the opposition thought about when the jury was sequestered, which Jean had somewhat touched upon earlier.

I wish I could have given voice to many others, but I was limited by the process, so I'm glad I gave voice to Joseph's mother, if I were to give it to anyone. Her presence and personal story show that, despite the tragic circumstances, she demonstrated the meaning of true courage and dignity. Of having grace.

Savages Triumph

How long the trial felt. Seemed years.
Watching the trial was like
watching the leaves of the kamani
trees do their slow twist in the wind,
the sun illuminating
the undersides, as if in a gathering of hope.
They would not be blown away.

To fill the long hours,
I crocheted mechanically,
and winced at the words:
rape, suspects, broken jaw,
an open but clean vagina.

I remember when my son once
brought me a plant on Arbor Day.
The leaves were young, deepening
in green, and I thought him good and kind,
my mother-soul trying to find evidence
of the meanness they accuse him of.

My Joe, did you really hit Mrs. Peeples?
My Joe, did you really rape Thalia Massie?
My Joe, in your goodness, did you really bring me a plant
that spread its branches
in translucent green sunbeams?

Were you capable of all this?

The green of a plant is a hopeful color.
What makes a rapist? Not the vegetation
around the boys who were purported
to have done the deed, the rustle
of the leaves and branches around them,
the breaking of twigs when
a woman was thrown from the car.
There is no evidence of any of this dirt
on her clothes or shoes.

I drop my wooden crochet needle.
It hits the floor with a dull *clack*
through the November that is here,
in the sticky humid winds of our winter.
It's still hurricane weather,
and the jury is finally sequestered.

I read the Bible and the newspapers.
The white people
in the gallery don't believe
I had been educated in the King's English,
and am highly literate,
but they continue to look down on me.
I can feel their eyes
and their hand-me-down hours
like everything I own.
Second-hand, not green and new.

Hung, they finally say:
Impossible to be in two places
at the same time,
the timeline wrong,
a lack of motive,
inconclusive evidence.

And it brings something else
into the surrounding air—
an emergent green feeling,
gratitude to a handful of brave good men,
a greening of the "savages"
the Japanese, Chinese, Portuguese, Filipinos,
and us, the natives, as we
begin to all come together.

Jean: Joseph's Perspective

This was the most difficult link to write. I'm trying to give voice to a dying man, an innocent man. I didn't know how to do it, but I felt that the voices of the accused had been lacking. But how to do it? What did they think? How did they feel? I read that Horace Ida was almost thrown off the Pali a few days before Kahahawai's killing. I could have written about that but I chose to concentrate on the murder. I imagined that these murderers sat around justifying their act as they drank.

> "... come together. . . in this together . . ."
> "... do justice . . ."
> " . . . jury wrong . . ."

Using a falsified summons, Mrs. Fortescue, Tommie Massie, and two others, Deacon Jones and Edward Lord, kidnapped Kahahawai as he emerged from the judiciary building after having reported to his probation officer. They drove him to Mānoa where they beat and tortured him trying to get a confession. Then someone shot him. (It was later determined that it was probably Deacon Jones.) It's speculated that he took a long time to die as he bled out, so I imagine him going in and out of consciousness. He heard the murderers but only in fragments. What I wanted to create is an antiphonal: the murderers' words and Kahahawai's hearing and lack of understanding. The murderers are repeating what they had read in the newspapers, that justice needed to be done, that the rapists were lust-driven youths, that forty rapes had occurred that year in Hawai'i. This was incorrect, but the mainland newspapers repeated these lies that sowed hysteria. Some even called for martial law.

To say the least, I didn't know whether it would work.

Another thing, when I saw the address of the murder house in Mānoa, I was dumbstruck. I drove past this street every day as a youngster.

Come Together

Jeez, their voices hurt my ears
my head is spinning
this floor is cold.
What they saying?

"…come together…in this together…"

"…do justice…"

"…jury wrong…"

"Confess, confess."

Auwe…what she talking
that Fortescue lady
so loud
they push me in the car
drag me here
I can't move

"…we're in this together…"

"…newspapers said…"

"…stop this chaos…"

"…lust-mad youths…
foul, slimy creatures…
attacking the innocent…"

"…forty rapes last year…"

"…martial law…"

What they talking?
Why they shoot me?

"Stay awake, Joey, stay awake?
Joseph! Don't go to sleep."

I hear you, Mommy,
I hear you
It's so hard

I don't want to die...

Christy: Local Perspective

I knew this was the poem I wanted to write at the beginning of this project, a poem to honor Joseph Kahahawai. In a ballsy move, Jean took the voice of a fading Kahahawai, which opened the door for me to write about his funeral. Fate.

I was comforted when reading of Kahahawai's funeral. Until then, reading this story was like eating razor blades. And then I learned that thousands came to Our Lady of Peace Cathedral to pay their respects. (I was baptized there.) I read the eloquence of the words of David Kama* in an unscheduled eulogy that said it directly, "these haoles murdered you in cold blood.... The truth will come out." I appreciated the *Star-Bulletin* printing Judge Robertson's letter which seriously questioned how the press was portraying Hawai'i and the trial of the accused, and a letter sent to the *New York Times* by former governor Wallace Farrington not only showing charges leveled by Admiral Stirling to be false but also suggesting that the men accused of the rape might well have been innocent. *Finally* I felt, *Finally*.

Early in the poem I start with a quote from Joseph:

> heart that never confessed
> *"I didn't do anything wrong, Daddy, I swear"*

This was actually a paraphrase from Joseph's father's eulogy where he shared the talks he had with his son during his incarceration awaiting the trial. Joseph fully denied all accusations against him, just as all the other boys did. It was important for me to start with his statement of innocence. It was the only words I felt bold enough to ascribe to him. I was fearful of misrepresenting Kahahawai or any of the accused so I didn't dare go there, as I had with supposing the voice of Thalia. But these words of defense, these words needed to be said.

I also specified in the poem:

> heart of a brown mother, heart of a brown father

While writing this, I felt it necessary to specify race, as race was crucial to Kahahawai's murder. Reading this poem independently, drawing attention to that, may or may not sit well with some readers. Within the context of this *renshi*, I stand by my decision.

The following list of what was lost, the items I attributed to Joseph came partly from what I read about him, and partly from my father's stories about what he used to do back when he lived down Akepo Lane.

> Not your eyes wide that took in boxing matches…
> Not your long-legged stride
> Not your shy laugh that lifted above this crooked path

Those were for Joseph.

> take you down to Akepo Lane
> past the pool hall's soft thud of a cushioned tip hitting the cue

That's my Pop; he was quite the pool hustler in his day.

> Take you to Kauluwela
> lean bodies gripping the dirt with toes—feet running, lunging, running.

That's for all the boys who were accused and all the boys growing up in Kalihi.

> Drive you along School Street—through A'ala Park
> past weathered old Filipinos shooting dice
> *"Boy, Boy, come!"*

That's for my grandpa, Basilio Passion, who was an immigrant that worked the sugar cane fields, until he got really good at playing cards—that's what I'm told anyway. The poem ends with a lyrical flourish meant to uplift, to pull us above all the bullshit. In a way, I felt somehow Joseph's death did that by bringing us together. I did not foresee writing it that way. The style is quite different from the preceding stanzas, but it came out naturally so I kept it. It was a gift.

* David Kama was a Hawaiian man whose brother, a police officer, was killed by an American soldier several years earlier.

To Die

You are not here.

Not your smooth skin taut over bones, over warm blood
coursing through your heart.
Heart of a brown mother, heart of a brown father
heart that never confessed
I didn't do anything wrong, Daddy, I swear

Not your eyes wide that took in boxing matches and light of a girl's face
not your fingers pulling through soft curls
not your long-legged stride
not your shy laugh that lifted above this crooked path.
Above the unease.
Not the bright memories that kept you whole:
high school dance, cousin's wedding, favorite black comb.
Not even the dark ones: haoles with rope.

And we who are here

do what we must: close the casket,
open the ground, return what was never ours and wonder—

can we take you once more, just once more,
to the places you loved? Go back—
carry you out of this field
bring your lei, your music

take you down to Akepo Lane
past the pool hall's soft thud of a cushioned tip hitting the cue.
Take you to Kauluwela
lean bodies gripping the dirt with toes—feet running, lunging, running.
Drive you along School Street—through A'ala Park
past weathered old Filipinos shooting dice
"Boy, Boy, come!"

Can we take you to the beginning?
back to the cradle when you were a babe
and could only look up; fat and drowsy
imagine not this world for us.
Imagine amazement,
slopes of green, bronze stars in the fishermen's net,
crack lightning in your tongue and veins—
all these within you pushing forward a reckless promise
that is inherent in every creation, Godlike. We.
Maybe there you can rise and let loose
the shame and fear inscribed in our palms

Ann: Admiral Stirling's Perspective

I love Christy's poem because it honored and respected Joseph Kahahawai as a son, a person. When Christy, Juliet, Jean, and I met, we shared our feelings of support for all the innocent men and their families. We also shared our knowledge of facts and history. Throughout the *renshi* poems, I did not write from the point of view of any of the innocent men in the Massie case. I included historical information in my poems to expose the actions of people who were hell-bent on persecution.

Grace Fortescue, Tommie Massie, Deacon Jones, and Edward J. Lord planned the kidnapping of Kahahawai that resulted in Kahahawai's murder. The following poem is in the point of view of Admiral Stirling.

As I read this poem, I think it accurately represents Stirling's mindset. It is a flawed mindset based on ideas of white superiority that justified putting other races in their place. It did not matter if a non-white person was innocent or guilty of a crime. If a person was not white, his/her life did not matter. This poem was hard to write since it has the erroneous point of view that murder was unavoidable and expected.

To make matters worse, the innocent men who were accused of raping Thalia Massie were in city jail for their safety while the white people who were involved in the murder of Kahahawai stayed on the USS *Alton*.

No Shame for Murder in 1932

What did Judd expect would happen?
Didn't he know that God-fearing men
protect their women when justice is not granted?

Judd is not fit to serve as governor.
I, Admiral Stirling, marched to 'Iolani Palace to explain to him
that mongrels accused of raping poor Thalia
must be protected in jail cells for their own good.
Otherwise, they may share the same fate as Kahahawai.

Did Judd believe there wouldn't be retribution?
No one could blame
a husband
a mother
and Navy brethren
who sought justice on their own terms.

How dare anyone attempt to jail these good white people?
Judge Christy allowed the Navy to have custody of our guests
aboard the USS *Alton* where they are protected and sheltered
with all the lodging and amenities they deserve.
They are blessed with flowers and messages inscribed with good wishes.

Juliet: Tommie Massie's Voice

On the timeline, it is already 1932, and after the trial for the murder of Joseph Kahahawai. Tommie Massie, Grace Fortescue, Deacon Jones, and Edward Lord, waiting to be sentenced, are incarcerated in fairly comfortable quarters on a boat in Pearl Harbor.

Ann's last line states: "They are blessed with flowers and messages inscribed with good wishes." From this line, my title became "We Are Blessed," with Tommie Massie as the narrator of this poem. How true this poem is, is unknown. Recently, I've thought deeply about changing the whole tenor of the poem because I was not sure if I had over-reached in my ideas. Did I have an ethical problem because I did not stick to the historical facts and had stretched my imagination, using poetic license, a tad too far? I'm not sure. Let me explain.

You will see, after reading the poem, I make two problematic assumptions: 1) that Tommie knows Thalia lied about the rape. It is true that she was beaten, but there had always been a question whether she was raped or not. And 2) that Thalia is not at all happy about Tommie and her mother murdering Kahahawai, believing they had gone too far.

My thoughts hinge on whether she lied or had not lied about the rape. If she did in fact lie, her mother, Tommie, and their accomplices had killed an innocent man in trying to protect the family's honor. If these assumptions were true, my contention is that both Thalia and Tommie were finding what they did difficult to live with. There is nothing to substantiate these speculations, but they may have some relationship to the real truth of what happened the night of Thalia's assault, and later, when Kahahawai was murdered.

Another problem with this poem is the profanity used. How do we present this to students? Do I have to create a sanitized version or self-select for different audiences? This has always been a quandary. There is always discomfort about this subject, especially with academicians and teachers. "Less is more," I was always told. While I worried about the language in this poem, after thinking about it, it felt more natural to use this language of castigation than to *not* use it. I wanted to show some of Tommie's anger and frustration in his denigration of Thalia. It also shows how psychotic both of them were.

We Are Blessed

with flowers and messages inscribed with good wishes,
and I think to myself what I really want to say to you
with captured words that never leave my imprisoned tongue.
Thalia, people across the nation agree I did
the right thing no matter what *you* believe.

We wait in this boat, as the government decides what to do with us,
its berths no different from jail cells, except for the privacy.
All day, every day, what are you sniveling about?
My whore wife, child, the whiff of you sickens me,
for you who are nothing but a fucking witch bitch,
who instigated with your cry of rape what we are enmeshed in,
which is not like the pranks we played in Patchogue.
This is real! And you pushed me to anger, like someone
pushes a kid from behind to do something he doesn't want to do.
Thus, I had to go through that dark tunnel and at its end,
fall off the cliff. During this whole time, I had to wonder
who you were—what hemlocks had you walked under,
what lilac branches had you snapped for your bouquets?
Under what sky, what waterfall?—especially when you actually
sully the very leaves you touch, the ground you walk on.
Thalia, Thalia, you dirty everything.

I often wondered about us, the forces that drove us—
your liquor, your mother, my honor—the unremitting anger
beneath my breastbone that swung like a pendulous knife
above our lives. Once set in motion, there was no turning back.

Lovely daughter, my once lovely wife.

No one knows better than I,
as to who or what you really are,
though I must admit you put on a good show,
walking with your head on a pike, looking hurt but avenged,
lifting eyes full of pride, crying with your handkerchief

up to your nose as if you are breathing in the fresh
scent of the white rose you hold. That's during the day,
in the light. But at night you're a different animal.
You don't touch me, save for the wine glass you suck
more tenderly than my manhood. How people would laugh
if they only knew. Whore/wife, I had to do what I did, don't you see?
How could I have done otherwise? Still hold my head high
among white people, like one must hold his head above water
to stay alive? Or die from shame? I could never be bested
by these savages, these niggers, who swam with you and slid
up and down your back on their surfboards, taking the waves to shore.
They could never be above or equal to us. So why
do you mourn what I did in your nightly pleadings?
Why? you ask, *why?* I did it for you, Thalia, for you!
You think I went too far. You hate me for it, don't you?
I can see it in your eyes.

Jean: Mainland Perspective

While Hawai'i was in turmoil, newspapers on the mainland churned up
sympathy for the Massies. Can you imagine this story today on CNN, Fox
News, and MSNBC for 24 hours a day? Crime in Paradise. Of course, in
1931 the coverage was different. First of all, alleged rapes wouldn't make the
headlines today, but the murder that followed might have. Even today it
would cause a sensation. In 1931 the story of five *coloreds* raping a white naval
officer's wife made headlines, yes, and then the trial for the murder of one of
the *coloreds*.

I was interested in how the people on the mainland felt about what was
happening here. It was disturbing to see—but not unexpected—that all the
sympathies lay with the Massies. When I saw that there was a call for martial law
in Hawai'i, I was shocked. This really must have been a time of turmoil similar
to that of Ferguson, Missouri, in 2014. Could there have been riots in Honolulu?
Well, there were near riots. For sure there would have been martial law, if people
had died in the streets.

I was ignorant of this part of Hawaii's history, a time when there might have been martial law, even before World War II (when it was declared after the bombing of Pearl Harbor). This ignorance probably was the cause of my not being able to figure out why there was so much resistance to statehood for Hawai'i in the 1960s. I don't remember anyone bringing up the Massie case. Of course, I may not have paid that much attention; nothing was on TV; I didn't read the papers; I wasn't much interested in the news. It was worldwide news in the 1930s, only obscured by the Lindberg kidnapping. People on the mainland believed there were race riots happening in the streets of Honolulu and that white women were being raped by the dozens. Forty assaults of all kinds reported in the police records were described as 40 rapes in the newspapers. There was only one reported rape in 1931. These are the kinds of headlines that were actually printed:

> "Honor Killing in Honolulu Threatens Race War"
> "Melting Pot of Peril"
> "Hawaii Crater of Racist Hate"
> "Many White Women Attacked"
> "Bayonets Rule Honolulu as Races Boil in Killing"

Senators called on President Hoover to declare martial law in Hawai'i because of this purported unrest and lawlessness. That he didn't is a credit to his getting the facts and not the fictions. But much had to be done to stem the tide of apparent hysteria here. All this happened before the trial against the murderers had even begun.

Maybe older people remember all the headlines during the Massie affair in the 1930s. But memories are short and people have died. My mother, born in 1920, only remembers the name, Massie case. It's a vague figment in our collective memory, though at that time it caused a sensation.

For my link I wanted to show what people on the mainland were thinking about Hawai'i as they read the newspapers. No television then. I thought about a typical couple looking at pictures in the papers and tsk-tsking the awful happenings, agreeing with the term "honor killing."

I Can See It in Their Eyes

Even in this grainy wedding picture
on the front page.
Look, Harry,
Aren't they so full of love?
Reminds me of when we were married.

What a shame! How can he look at her in the same way
now after the rape?

The News calls it "Honor Killing,"
they felt they had to do it.
My brother says the *Louisville Herald* is carrying the story too.
Must be all over the country, maybe all over the world.

Are you listening, Harry?

Look, here's another picture,
that rapist, Horace Ida.
Look at those slant eyes.
Says here all the trouble in Hawai'i is a Jap plot .

There sure were a lot of Japs in Hawai'i
when we were there on vacation.
Remember? Strange eyes.

My brother says there's a danger of them being tried
by a jury of yellow men for the killing of a yellow man.
That's not right. Doesn't the Constitution say a jury of
equals?

Looks like there's race wars in Hawai'i,
Not a place for decent people.

No wonder they're asking President Hoover to
declare martial law.

You could say that's the end of paradise.

Christy: Deacon Speaks

This poem is anachronistic, but there was no way I was going to let this link go forward without somehow addressing Deacon, the man who shot Joseph Kahahawai. Let me refresh the timeline a little bit.

Tensions escalated during the rape trial and after the eventual mistrial. Navy wives were complaining of being treated without respect or even being threatened by locals. A hoax perpetuated by petty officers aimed at stirring up tensions further (a fabricated note suggesting more of "your women" will be raped and signed, "The Kalihi Gang") did just that. Riots were breaking out between the Navy enlisted and local men. An edition of the *Honolulu Times* entitled "Shame of Honolulu" not only exacerbated these fears, but also printed the addresses of the accused men, making them targets. Shortly thereafter, Horace Ida was abducted and beaten severely by sailors. It was during this time that Deacon Jones, a Navy machinist, was given the detail to serve as protection for Thalia while Tommie was away on duty.

Deacon Jones was a twelve-year Navy veteran, a boxing trainer who had lived in the South. Deacon and Grace got along well, sharing the same sense of humor and outlook. It was during this time, in the aftermath of the mistrial, that a plan to kidnap and force a confession out of Kahahawai was hatched between Deacon, Grace, and Tommie. They never got a confession out of him.

My first attempt at writing in Deacon's voice was ridiculous. It was filled with dated slang and a bravado that came across as phony. I reread Stannard and reviewed an interview with Deacon that took place after the Kahahawai murder trial. During the interview Deacon readily admits to being the one who shot Kahahawai. Unlike the Thalia poem that was more about "emotional truth" versus historical fact, I was much more concerned with putting real details in this piece.

> Not like a reckoning, not like how
> your mother preached at you
> 'bout the thunderstorms coming

I was hoping the word choice and dialect would allude to Deacon's Southern connection.

> Tommie was a boy of books and words
> and words and empty hands

During the interview Deacon states Tommie never carried a gun, and that he was a very educated boy. The intimation of these words along with other excerpts impressed upon me that Deacon did not think Tommie man enough to get his hands dirty.

> That nigger was no fool

Both Deacon and Grace are on record as referring to Kahahawai as "nigger." There is also a direct quote by Deacon (referring to Kahahawai) "and this guy was no fool."

> I paid attention to his wide nose
> and the line of his jaw, was ready when
> his eyes turned angry.

In the interview Deacon reveals that he saw Kahahawai's body language change from fear to "getting his nerve back."

> Even after Tommie left
> the air stayed thick, refusing to rise
> what can you do about it?
> Shit needed attention
> the bathroom floor needed mopping

Tommie left to dispose of the body. Deacon stayed behind to clean up the mess. In the interview I learned hat they put his body in the bathtub as a result of Deacon's false logic that water would draw the blood out of his body.

> My stomach growled
> so I tossed back a few more

Deacon began drinking once Tommie left. When the cops came a few hours later to investigate the scene, Deacon was drunk.

> I push the bloody towels to the side
> and find the bullet shell, shove it deep
> in my pocket, necessary, when the phone rings;
> *the cops are coming*

At the station, the police search Deacon and find an empty bullet shell in his pants pocket. In his underwear, they find a magazine clip and the false summons created by Grace Fortescue and used to lure Kahahawai to the car before abducting him.

I wanted the tone of this piece to be of reluctant acceptance, to be on the verge of something and not knowing if it was going to be good or bad. I was hoping it would come across as a bit of rumination, but whether it did or not, I could not bypass the opportunity to tell everyone that Deacon did it.

You Could Say
(Deacon's lament)

You could say
it was a long time coming.
Not like a reckoning, not like how
your mother preached at you
'bout the thunderstorms coming
after she caught you behind the shed
fucking the neighbor girl
bare ass in the air
but more like,
a wakening,
a moment that the roads lead to,
and you know it, know it
in your belly that something
necessary is going to happen.

I wanted to tell Tommie *Don't be afraid*
but the day was just too damn hot,

the heat was swollen in my mouth.
Tommie was a boy of books and words
and words and empty hands.
That nigger was no fool,
I paid attention to his wide nose
and the line of his jaw, was ready when
his eyes turned angry. *Tommie,*
words ain't gonna work on this.

Even after Tommie left
the air stayed thick, refusing to rise
what can you do about it?
Shit needed attention
the bathroom floor needed mopping
and spots of blood where the good carpet
used to be, was shouting his name.
My stomach growled
so I tossed back a few more,
I remember thinking you can swallow
fear as much as you can swallow good
and they mostly go down the same.

I push the bloody towels to the side
and find the bullet shell, shove it deep
in my pocket, necessary, when the phone rings;
the cops are coming

It's all come down to this.

Ann: Darrow's Voice

This poem is in the point of view of Clarence Darrow. As an attorney, Clarence
Darrow would attempt to represent his clients (defendants accused of Kahahawai's
murder) successfully. He would also present himself in the best possible light. In
this poem, I referenced Stannard and included Darrow's trial history and money
issues. I asked myself, how would Darrow justify being the defense attorney for this
case? Then, I wrote this poem.

It's All Come to This

Let's face it, the money's good,
and I wanted to travel to Hawai'i.
I can't believe my life's work has come to this—
I need to sit down.

I wanted to retire when I was fifty,
but I kept working due to disappointing investments.
All those trials:
Leopold and Loeb,
Scopes,
Sweet.
Finally, at seventy-one,
I had enough money to retire.
Then, the '29 crash hit.
How could I have prepared?
My son is in debt; I lost a lot.

Luckily, people know my name, and it helps.
Working with Universal Pictures
and participating in public arguments on religion
brought in money—
for a while.
Now people rather spend their money on the talkies.

All my years of fighting for the rights of blacks—
to have it come to this:
I received a cable with the prospect of defending
Mrs. Grace Fortescue and three men
who killed a native Hawaiian man.
They're paying a good price for my services.

Barnes can't believe I'm here.
My wife says I can do good work in Hawai'i
and help everyone get along,
but I know she doesn't feel right about any of this.

I know what some people are thinking, and I don't blame them.
How could Clarence Darrow be attorney for the defense?

Juliet: People's Voice

How could Clarence Darrow? I wanted to show "he could" because he was Clarence Darrow, one of the more famous lawyers of his time, who, nevertheless, had been controversial in many of the cases he defended. The murder of Joseph Kahahawai by Grace Fortescue et al. may have been another of the many high profile cases he had handled, but it was also the case that questioned his integrity the most because he was clearly on the wrong side of the situation. Three of the suspects were caught with the body of Kahahawai before they could dispose of it. His entering the case was very much a "What some people would do for money!" situation. In the end, it was a sad commentary on Darrow's life and legacy.

When I first saw the movie *Inherit the Wind*, starring Spencer Tracy, I thought I found a hero in Clarence Darrow. At the time, I did not know anything about Thalia Massie's supposed rape and the subsequent murder of Kahahawai. But later, when I read about what happened, I was very disappointed that Darrow took the job of lawyer for the defense. It was irksome to think how he tried to get the killers off by calling on two psychologists to say that Tommie was temporarily insane and had murdered Kahahawai because of his love for Thalia.

It is clear Darrow agreed to be the lawyer for the defense because he needed the money. But what else motivated him to take this case at the end of his famous career? What made him willing to take on a case that might tarnish an overall decent legacy forever? It is well known he wanted to help his son who had fallen into financial difficulty and lost everything in the stock market crash of October 1929. But it seems he also needed money for his own indulgences, his dalliances, and creature comforts. Whether he won his last case or not, he knew he was going to be well paid.

Darrow was a complicated man. In Hawai'i, people would have described him as someone having a "swift mouth." Exactly. People in Hawai'i at the time probably could not help but question how the prosecution was going to go against someone this famous, this glib, who could argue for hours. Going against Darrow appeared daunting. Little did he know, however, that the prosecution was equally motivated for the right causes and reasons. The lawyers for the prosecution, John Kelley and his assistant Barry Urlich, and the presiding judge Albert Christy, need to be commended for their right-mindedness and righteous views. Brave jurors who put their jobs and homes on the line because they were on the wrong side of the military and financially powerful elites in Hawai'i, should also be applauded.

The conditions and circumstances show that all Darrow cared for was money, and my poem brings it to this sorry conclusion. After studying his role in the case, I ended up feeling sorry for him. The murder of Kahahawai brought a sad ending to an illustrious career that fell into obscurity.

At this time, I have to admit I was tired of thinking about the rape case, about Thalia Massie, Grace Fortescue, Tommie Massie and his friends. I was also disappointed in Darrow's role and jaded by how he plotted to get his clients off. To think that this even happened was too demoralizing. While he did lose the case, which was a good and just thing, those convicted of the murder had their 10-year sentences commuted by Governor Lawrence Judd, whose excuse was that he was pressured by those in Washington. This was almost enough to make me want to throw up my hands and give up!

I confess I did not write anything much about Darrow because there is so much written and found on the Internet about his life and all the cases he handled and their outcomes, many of them famous but often controversial, like the figure he had been.

How Could Clarence Darrow?

Because the law gave him an ethical basis to hide behind money—
defend the indefensible, assail the unassailable—he could.

It is April. The day is warm on the day of the trial, the smell
of coffee fills the halls and for the exhilaration this brings—he could.

To save a son staggering in debt, for his own comfort,
to indulge his wife's extravagances, to pamper his lover—he could.

Notwithstanding being the champion of Blacks,
hero of the Scopes trial and Sweet case—he could.

For the same reasons he was defense attorney
for Leopold and Loeb, even for attorneys caught bribing jurors—he could.

While a hero of the downtrodden, he infamously defended the owners
who had locked 29 of 30 exits of the Iroquois Theater fire. 506 died.

A chameleon, forever opportunistic, he changed like the seasons,
or the hands of a clock. A master of camouflage, he could change

from the righteous, the rod and staff, to the reproachable,
fire and brimstone, or like the brown praying mantis, into a leaf,

to catch its prey for the *green* he loved best.

Jean: About John Kelley, Prosecutor

I liked writing this link the best, because I had found a hero: John Kelley. When I
went to the Hawai'i archives, I was really moved by something he wrote in a memo:
"Righteousness does not come only in one color. Men of good conscience tried to
do right."

I felt like a detective, trying to put together a life in a few words. "Just the facts,
ma'am, just the facts." Stannard provided a good thumbnail biography of Kelley,
which gave me a flavor of the man. Like the proverbial Irishman, Kelley loved
to drink. That was exactly what I needed to hook Juliet's last line to my link.
Unfortunately the only green alcoholic drink I know is that powerfully sweet
liqueur, Chartreuse. It's not really a man's drink, let alone for someone like Kelley.
But I had no choice. I had to get the green into the link. This is the only fictional
detail I included in the poem.

Kelley came from Butte, Montana, and after traveling the Pacific settled in
Hawai'i. A brilliant and hard-working Republican lawyer, he defended unions
and was a partner in a firm full of Democrats, which included William Heen,

one of the defense lawyers in the rape case. Stannard slyly notes the irony of Kelley's brother, Cornelius, who being a Democrat in Montana, spent his time busting unions.

Kelley was a relative neophyte, almost 30 years younger than Clarence Darrow, who must have been the best-known lawyer in the U.S. at that time. I imagined a battle, a fight, and the word "face-off" came to mind.

> After all, he has a face-off with Darrow,
> that expert of the sleight of hand

Stannard used the term "sleight of hand" to indicate a "master of indirection" which led me to "magician."

> He knew he was up against the magician

I found it interesting that in the 1930s the insanity defense didn't often work, but Darrow was going to use it. It seemed odd to me that the medical specialists, today's psychiatrists, were called "alienists." I guess it's because they dealt with the alienated. Even more peculiar, to me at least, was the term for "temporary insanity" which was rendered as "alarm clock" insanity. Language is funny.

> who would probably call in alienists to argue the
> "alarm clock" insanity—it's only temporary—as a defense.

The story about the toilet was one of the most outrageous details I found in Stannard's account of the trial. It really enraged me. But it typifies the patrician attitudes of people like Mrs. Fortescue. After all, they had separate toilets in the South at this time. Mrs. Fortescue could not put her ass on the same seat as the plebeians, so a separate staircase was built (can't meet anyone going there), as well as a lounge, kitchenette, and powder room at a cost of $3,007.50. All this privilege while she was on trial for killing Kahahawai.

I had a kick using the word "hoi polloi" for the internal rime with toilet, as it reflected her attitude towards the masses. The last line came to me in a flash:

This makes him thirst. He'll need a flood of drink after the trial,
one that would flush it all away.

The Green He Loved Best

The green he loved best was the velvety
color of that drink he had. Where was it anyway—
China? Australia? Fiji?—the one with
the name he couldn't pronounce. "The green one,
you know," he'd say to the bartender.
Not like any drink he had with his brother in Butte,
to wash away the copper dust from those Montana mines.

But now in Hawai'i it was not time for a binge
not for John Kelley, prosecutor, not now.
Now was the time for butt-off work.
After all, he'll have a faceoff with Darrow,
that expert of the sleight of hand,
with 30 years experience over him.
He knew he was up against the magician,
who would probably call in alienists to argue the
"alarm clock" insanity—it's only temporary—as a defense.
Or he'll pull the empathy cord. What would you do
in their place? You'd have to defend her honor.

Kelley knows that any trial is over when jury selection is complete.
Could a white jury convict? he wonders.

Then he thinks of the "powder room" with lounge and separate entry
they built for Mrs. Fortescue because, of course, she couldn't use the same
toilet as the hoi polloi.

This makes him thirst. He'll need a flood of drink after the trial,
one that would flush it all away.

Christy: Esther's Perspective about the Trial

I remember being of two minds when I came to this point in the project. On the one hand, I felt the links were being pushed forward too quickly; there were too many aspects both big and small that were being neglected, too much untold. While on the other hand, just as my fellow writers admitted, this process was exhausting. Ruminating, considering, and attaching yourself to both people and a time whose stories are unchangeable, whose injustice you cannot correct, and whose pain you cannot comfort, was for me, grueling.

What did we miss? The partial list: All the accused and the time they were incarcerated for "their safety," their lives on hold. How did they react to Horace's beating? To Joseph's murder? To the newspaper stories? To the trials? Governor Judd and every decision he made that led up to this point (I'm not sure what was more of an injustice, Deacon getting away with murder or that Governor Judd never had to answer for his decisions that allowed it to happen). Dillingham's collusion with Stirling; the newspaper editors locally and on the mainland; the fathers of the five men accused; military wives who knew Thalia and those who didn't; Beatrice Nakamura, the Massie's maid who had both access and insight. All this is some of what we missed.

The sets of poems that followed my Deacon link focused on the attorneys for both the prosecution and the defense. I brought it back to a mother's voice, the mother of Joseph Kahahawai, Esther Anito. Just as I needed to write about Kahahawai's funeral and I needed to name Deacon. I also had a need to present Esther. She lost the most.

I couldn't relate to her immense loss so, as with the Stirling poem, I had to rely on form to give the reader a sense of her. The form of the pantoum builds on repeating lines in specific sequence. This repetition gives impact and also unfolds in a metered way. If successful, I would unveil her in a way that spoke to her strength.

There were several key elements of Esther's brief time on the witness stand that made an impression on me. One of them was her manner of dress, a white kīkepa that gave her a formal demeanor.

She wore a white kīkepa to the stand

A kīkepa is a length of fabric, traditionally made of tapa (cloth made from bark), worn by wrapping it under one arm and tying it over the shoulder of the opposite arm. I think of Hawaiian activists marching in protest wearing kīkepa; in that instance, the kīkepa (for me) exudes not only a regal aspect, but also portrays revolution and strength in identity. In my mind, I see no difference in Esther's march to the stand and Hawaiian activists marching in front of 'Iolani Palace. I can see her conviction while tying the knot of the cloth over her shoulder that morning when she dressed. I know this kīkepa was her shield. I know her every breath, movement, and decision about that day was a fight for justice, for her son.

How many children did she have?
Two children, Joseph and Lillian
No one in the courtroom breathed
listening as she gave it all away

She remembered two children, Joseph and Lillian
But is Joseph alive? A mother's cry

This was a heartbreaking element for me, her stumble when the prosecution asked how many children she had. Esther had four children; two had died at an early age. She initially made the mistake of saying she had two children alive then corrected herself. Her voice, in the correction of that statement, came across as a faint wail. Esther did not break down on the stand. She was reported to have held herself with dignity. I cry at McDonald's commercials, I cannot imagine this kind of strength.

And that strength did not fail her when the prosecution asked her to identify Joseph's bloodstained shirt. What struck me was not the fact that she had to identify the shirt in its gruesome state, but rather that she had lovingly mended it the night before so he could look his best for his appointment the next day.

Joseph's bloodstained shirt on display
her hands instinctively reach out to it
she sees the mending from the night before
proof that she took care of her son

We place expectations in the small tasks that we do, that they will carry forward, do their intention, and be forgotten. Filling the ice cube tray, sweeping the porch, folding towels and putting them away, all are things we do without thought. These smallest of things, like sewing buttons onto a shirt, should never be the final marker of such a monumental event as the death of your son.

Gave It All Away

She wore a white kīkepa to the stand
quiet when the prosecution found it necessary to ask
Objection, objection! came from the defense
but the judge nodded for her to reply

The prosecution found it necessary to ask
how many children she had
The judge nodded for her to reply
and no one in the courtroom moved

How many children did she have?
Two children, Joseph and Lillian
No one in the courtroom breathed
listening as she gave it all away

She remembered two children, Joseph and Lillian
But is Joseph alive? A mother's cry
the tremble in her voice gave it all away
The jurors strained to hear

No, Joseph is not alive. A mother confronts
the bloodstained shirt on display
while the jurors strain to hear how
she mended it the night before

Joseph's bloodstained shirt on display
her hands instinctively reach out to it,
she sees the mending from the night before
proof that she took care of her son

She instinctively reaches out to him
lets the tears fall as the prosecution rests

proves she is still taking care of her son
enduring in her white kīkepa to the stand

Ann: About the Trial

The events of the Massie and Kahahawai cases are heartbreaking. Christy included the strength of Joseph Kahahawai's mother in her poem. For more information on the trial, I returned to Stannard. During the trial, Clarence Darrow included information regarding Thomas Massie's mental state due to his wife's assault. Darrow wanted a sympathetic jury that would understand that Kahahawai's death was inevitable under the circumstances. John Kelley, the prosecuting attorney, wanted the jury to focus on the facts of the case and the murder of Kahahawai. The trial resulted in a guilty verdict with a reduced one-hour sentence.

Later, the Pinkerton report admitted that all men accused of raping Thalia Massie were innocent, and charges were dropped. The report also mentioned that there was not enough evidence to support that Thalia Massie was raped.

As we read these facts, it is clear that there was a witch-hunt to persecute the innocent men who did not rape Thalia Massie, and the reduced one-hour sentence for Kahahawai's murder is still an outrage. History vindicates and sides with the persecuted victims of these cases: Horace Ida, Ben Ahakuelo, Joseph Kahahawai, Henry Chang, and David Takai.

I'm writing this commentary in 2016. In the continental United States, there still is a sense of entitlement and fear. Instead of valuing diversity, some believe it is a threat. The voice of racism, sexism, xenophobia, homophobia, and other forms of fear and hate gains momentum and strength as it battles with common sense and logic. We have witnessed this before. We must not repeat horrific historical events. We must realize that equality and diversity are strengths, so we can unite and solve the world's problems together.

To the Stand

Clarence Darrow called Thomas Massie to the stand
to show how his wife's assault and related events thereafter
affected his mental state and resulted in Kahahawai's death.

Psychiatric authorities testified, and Thalia testified
on how her circumstances affected Tommie.

Darrow pondered during his closing argument:
What would anyone do in this situation?
What if you were the husband or mother of Thalia?

For the prosecution, John Kelley's closing argument was simple:
A man was murdered.
What if you were the mother of Joseph Kahahawai?

Juliet: Esther's Voice and Grace's Voice

Part I: *Of Joseph Kahahawai*

What if you were the mother of Joseph Kahahawai? Yes, what if? How would you
have reconciled the senseless killing of your son? How would you be able to go
about your daily life, knowing this awful fact? That's why I began writing this
poem. I wanted to explore Esther Anito's grief and show how it affected her. While
a loss is a loss, Joseph's death must have been especially heart-wrenching for it was
utterly unnecessary.

It is difficult to deal with any death in the family, even under ordinary
circumstances like illness or old age. I know a grief such as what Esther Anito
and the Kahahawai family had encountered would never disappear because of its
tragic nature. In addition, the family members would have had to deal with its
continuing reverberation, reminders surfacing when similar situations crop up
every so often in the community. It is understandable that they may have wanted
to keep what had happened buried in the private layer of their lives. And poetry,
especially because of its revelatory nature, in its delving into the human condition

and emotional landscape, could cause unwarranted feelings to resurface or bring about renewed discomfort by reflecting on events that took place in 1931 and 1932. My intention in writing this poem, however, was not to cause additional grief or to debase Joseph's memory, but to *honor* it.

I believe I achieved this goal in the first part of the poem, by showing that while grief was always there for Esther, over time, the grief changed in form for her, becoming a source of solace rather than that of deep pain. It must have been especially hard for her whenever her son's murder was brought up, similar to what we are doing right now. I, and the other poets working on this project, have tried to remain respectful and sensitive at all times. Nevertheless, I would like to think of Joseph's family as resilient and am hopeful that, despite our intrusion into their lives, our writing about the case and the deep abiding hurt of Joseph's death would be lessened by what our poems illuminate.

Part II: *Of Thalia Massie*

Unfortunately, I did not achieve similar clarity writing about Grace Fortescue's grief because I was *overly* sympathetic, when I shouldn't have been, about her grief over Thalia's suicide. Let me elaborate further. Part II has Grace looking back on Thalia's suicide as an old woman and saying:

> ...I can tell you that my pain and
> suffering never ceased.
> Who is to know another's suffering?
> For retribution comes one way
> or another. I learned this
> too late... In the end, however,
> I endured a greater sentence—
> a life sentence of regret and remorse.

Thinking about what I had written, I firmly believe I gave Grace too much credit, as to how a normal person under such circumstances would feel. And this is where I believe I made my error when writing about her, for she was in no way *normal*.

For instance, I have her saying: "I can tell you that my pain and/suffering never ceased...." This is probably what a normal person might feel. But knowing something about the coldness of her character, I cannot help but think that the pain of her daughter's death was short-lived. I go on to say:

> ...Who is to know another's suffering?
> for retribution comes one way
> or another.

Yes, no one can really know Grace's suffering. What sort of retribution was I thinking suitable for her? Looking back upon her life, I have to say my words run counter to the life she led after her commutation, as well as after Thalia's suicide.

Initially, Thalia's death probably did bring about suffering for Grace, but understanding something of her hardness, I could not see her suffering very long after her daughter's suicide. I can't help but think she may in fact have been *relieved* by Thalia's death after her much troubled life. After that, could not Grace go on with her own life in comfort? Much of her life after her daughter's suicide points toward this.

What is more in keeping with Grace's character is that she says she was never repentant or remorseful:

> Never for killing Kahahawai, however,
> I still have a cold heart where he's concerned

This is one area she has never backed down on, always thinking of him as one of the perpetrators of Thalia's alleged rape. She then goes on to say after Thalia's suicide:

> I have to admit. I shared the same
> grief as Joseph Kahahawai's mother,
> for wasn't I as passionate a mother
> as she had been when Thalia was brutalized?

While I have her saying this in the poem, I don't really think she makes the leap presented. Just this lack of understanding about the hurt she feels for the loss of her daughter, thinking that it could ever be similar to the sorrow and hurt Esther felt for the loss of Joseph, shows a deficiency evident in the depth of her feelings, as I found in my readings about her.

In much of what has been written about her background and life, Grace has often been portrayed as a foolish, conniving, selfish woman. It also sounds as if, before and after Thalia's death, she went about her life as if home free, without a heavy burden of guilt regarding the events that took place in Hawai'i. As Christy says in her first commentary: "I needed to know that justice would prevail. I needed something bad to happen to the people who did really bad things. But for the most part it didn't. Thalia's suicide years later was the closest I would get." I got what Christy said. I too have marveled at people who do terrible things and still live long, comfortable lives, as though they had done nothing wrong. We've all heard of people like this, haven't we? It is safe to say Esther Anito never had this luxury.

What bothered me most about the second part of my last poem? I did not want readers to think that I was in any way sympathetic to Grace's plight. I truly was not trying to be sympathetic, for her sorrow was misplaced. I wanted readers to see that her sorrow was not at the same level as that of Esther's, that it was weak and skewed in nature. Having said that, I believe I failed to adequately illustrate the difference between Esther's grief and Grace's. I failed to adequately expose Grace's flippant, steely manner about Kahahawai's murder. I failed to adequately depict how the aftereffect of her son's death followed Esther, while the aftereffect of Thalia's death had little impact on Grace. I failed to adequately portray how very different these two women were in temperament. I failed to adequately reveal how much more terrible Kahahawai's death had been in its injustice, as opposed to Thalia's suicide. I failed to adequately show... I failed to adequately show....

I know I could have changed the whole poem, but in many ways, I wanted to leave it to illustrate something of a writer's dilemma. I guess I could have gone on to rewrite it, but again time had been of the essence and only after doing the commentaries for these poems did I realize the conundrum I was faced with. This has been a good writing lesson. The project itself a life lesson.

What If You Were the Mother?

Of Joseph Kahahawai

I would grieve all my life.
Though the grieving would change over the years,
the angry shark of it that attacked my gut,
lessening its hold on me in time.

But I can guarantee you one thing.
Every morning when I wake up,
something of it would be back at my doorstep
like the old familiar neighborhood stray cat
let in to curl at my side for the rest of the day.

And this grief would well up
at odd moments in my life.
When I see the face of a child at the window
looking out, or a boy on his bike,
cards between the spokes,
making sounds in the wind.

Or, at a sudden rain, splattering
its droplets
upon the roof of my memory.

It would serve as a memento—
the stone I carry in my pocket,
the golden locket I hang around my neck.

This grief would rise up in me
when I see a rainbow or the setting sun,
or when I smell his shirt still hanging
in the closet and, once in a while, take
up to my face. Be overcome
by his scent. I would drop to my knees
and fall to the floor and slap
the hard dark wood with my hands
while I would scold myself: "Don't do this!"
I will never stop.

I wouldn't be able to help myself,
grief the only way to be closest to him.

Of Thalia Massie

Looking back at this mess,
as an old woman,
I can tell you that my pain and
suffering never ceased.
Who is to know another's suffering?
For retribution comes one way
or another. I learned this
too late,
despite my triumphant release,
the commutation, the one-hour sentence
I spent drinking champagne.
In triumph? Perhaps. In the end, however,
I endured a greater sentence—
a life sentence of regret and remorse.
Never for killing Kahahawai, however.
I still have a cold heart where he's concerned
for I believe he was the perpetrator.
But for the pain I felt for my daughter
as I watched her plummet
as if from the cliffs of the Pali,
becoming an alcoholic, a drug addict,
and at the end, someone who tried
to commit suicide once, twice,
succeeding on the second try,
her body found in some cheap hotel room.

I have to admit. I shared the same
grief as Joseph Kahahawai's mother,
for wasn't I as passionate a mother
as she had been when Thalia was brutalized?
Wasn't our suffering the reason for Tommie's and my
wanting to murder her son in the first place?

Thalia's suffering, my suffering,
Thalia's pain, my pain,
her death, my death.
I was heartbroken when I went to collect
her body and bury her in the cold
hard ground so far away from your angry
shores where the ripples of outrage
continue throughout the years.

Jean: The Poet Speaks

I saw Juliet's last line and thought, "Thank you, Juliet."

When we began writing this *renshi*, I knew next to nothing about Massie-Kahahawai. After reading, thinking, and writing about this period of time, I was less ignorant than before, but...forgetting is so easy. So I started this link with a series of "we'll forget..." and ended with the question "what must we remember?"

In November 2011, while we were in the midst of the *renshi*, something terrible happened. A 27-year-old haole from the mainland, here to work for the Bureau of Diplomatic Security, shot and killed a 23-year-old Hawaiian in a Waikīkī McDonald's. The case has still not been resolved.

A few days ago—July 8, 2016— an African American veteran of the Iraq wars killed five police officers and wounded many others, including African Americans who were demonstrating for Black Lives Matter. We were told that he acted because he was sick and tired of seeing black men killed by the police. This occurred after two black men, one in Minnesota and the other in Louisiana, were shot down by police. And then again yesterday, three policemen were killed and others wounded. I sit here numb.

It is clear that racial tension, the sense of being wronged, whether on one side or the other, must be at the heart of all this violence. That heart seems empty and bitter. What can we remember that might help to prevent similar actions based on fear, hatred, and loss, motivated by desires for retribution and justice? Is there justice anywhere?

As a non-white, non-black, I could have felt invisible, maybe spared from all this since my color gets absorbed in other people's spectrum and, more importantly, because I have lived in Hawai'i for most of my life. But people like Admiral Stirling pointedly used racial discrimination in calling Japanese members of that "orange" race. Such recurring labels won't let me fade out of sight. Fortunately, I've experienced racism only in small, non-violent ways. For example, once in Merced, California, I was denied service in a Woolworth cafe. Not much to complain about.

The most anxiety causing experience I've ever had was when my husband was hauled into a Costa Mesa, California police station for suspicion of attempted kidnapping. He was picked up while jogging on a street. When he explained that he didn't drive (was he going to carry the woman on his back?) the officer still insisted that my husband go with him to the station. Later I learned from an African student that the police there routinely harassed blacks. I count myself lucky to live in Hawai'i.

What I want to remember about the Massie-Kahahawai story is that people of different backgrounds had a sense of what I believe is justice and tried to prevent injustice from happening. I think of the defense team for the local boys who were from different ethnic backgrounds. I think of the jury made up of men of all colors who had much to lose but did not find the boys guilty. I think of the judge who persuaded the grand jury to charge the Fortescue group for murder. I think of the prosecutor of the murderers, John Kelley.

One of my French-African literature students, a haole from the mainland, confessed to me one day that even though she had been subject to racist remarks, she was glad, yes glad, to have come to the University of Hawai'i because she now knew how it felt to be in someone else's shoes, to be the object of someone else's prejudice, and this education she would never have had on the mainland. She was serious; for her it was life-changing. In Hawai'i everyone can be the object of somebody else's prejudice. She wasn't the only mainland student to make this remark to me. Of course, there were others who told me that Hawai'i was the most racist state they had ever lived in and wanted to leave as soon as possible.

Before I went to study abroad, I don't think I ever had an African American classmate in any of my classes, from kindergarten until junior year in France. So I had little experience with Negroes—that's the polite term that I had been taught to use. I thought I was free from prejudice. My error became apparent when I was registering for classes at the University of California at Irvine and a tall, black figure approached me. Instinctively, I jerked back, out of his way, even though he wasn't that near me. He looked at me and glared. At first I was surprised that I had jumped, then I felt embarrassed. I was made physically conscious of my own fear. This was something I didn't know about myself.

Where did that suspicion and fear come from?

For decades I would visit my maternal grandparents in Kōloa plantation's Japanese camp. As a child I didn't think about who was living where. All I knew was that everyone around me was Japanese. Only later did I find out that there was a Filipino camp. I never knew why we were separated like that until I read somewhere that separation by races helped the plantation control the workers. By keeping families apart and unfamiliar with each other, suspicions and fears could thrive, thus preventing unity. We were living in silos, cultural ghettos.

Stannard describes the funeral of Joseph Kahahawai as a notable moment when one saw among the mostly Hawaiian crowd large numbers of Japanese, Chinese, other Asians, and even a group of haole. These people united as a community of mourners. Pain brought them together. It has been suggested that a sense of mutuality emerged from these events.

As people from different groups left the plantation and mingled and tried to find some way to live together in the community, I imagine they had to find ways to joke with each other. If tears can bind, so can laughter. I died laughing every time I heard Rap Reiplinger sing his song to Faith Yanagi to the tune of "Tell Laura I Love Her." Even though it hurt when Frank De Lima made his slant eyes and spoke with buckteeth, I laughed at his caricatures of Japanese. It was all right. He did it to everybody. It saddens me that some of us have lost our sense of humor. I'm grateful that one of the truisms my mother repeated to me was "Sticks and stones can break my bones but words can never hurt me." That saved me from many a fight and toughened me.

We in Hawai'i are lucky that we can all experience being the object of someone else's prejudice. We learn to live with it, and until recently we were able to laugh in public about it. This is what being local has meant to me. We accept each other. This is part of what my student was alluding to. Like a mixed plate lunch, we have mixed plate pain and laughter.

Many decades ago during the race riots in Watts, one of my classmates told me that her family had to move to Canada from Madagascar. Why? I asked. Because they were Chinese and not Madagascan. Weren't you born there? I asked. Yes, she answered, but everyone not native had to leave. I was born in Hawai'i and always thought I belonged here. What if...? I wondered. Where would I go?

I'm not Hawaiian, but Hawai'i is my home. Some say I am a guest. Yes...but, what does that mean? I read with relief that Queen Lili'uokalani welcomed the Japanese, in fact all peoples, and even made them citizens of Hawai'i. This prompted me to write these lines in my poem, "Mai Poina" (Don't Forget):

> I think of you,
> Lili'uokalani, and of your people,
> the *kanaka maoli*,
> and of your uprightness towards us
> of different colors,
> born here and
> come from other places.

I know that Hawai'i is not that joy zone perpetuated by the tourist industry. We are a complex society with complicated relationships and feelings, conflicted feelings. I often ask myself—especially when it concerns things defined as "native"—does my opinion count on matters about Hawai'i? especially when it concerns things defined as "native?" It reminds me of a talk that I heard at UH when Ngũgĩ wa Thiong'o, a Kenyan writer, came to give a lecture about post-colonialism. During the Q&A, a Hawaiian student complained about non-Hawaiians who were signing up to learn Hawaiian. She thought that this was yet another example of people trying to steal from the Hawaiians. In his wisdom, Ngũgĩ said he would be happy if other people wanted to learn his language because it would mean its survival. To me the voyages of the Hōkūle'a demonstrate that kind of Hawaiian spirit.

So how did I get here from Massie-Kahahawai? There is something here about our learning to live together, something in the idea that time metes out its own justice and humankind must forgive. Queen Liliʻuokalani wrote it in the "The Queen's Prayer" (published in *He Buke Mele Hawaii*):

> Mai nānā ʻinoʻino
> Nā hewa o kānaka,
> Akā e huikala,
> A maʻemaʻe nō.

> Oh! look not on their failings,
> Nor on the sins of men,
> Forgive with loving kindness,
> That we might be made pure.

Through the Years

we'll forget the dates and details of the alleged rape;

we'll forget the green silk dress, the names of the accused, Tin Can Alley, the make of the car;

we'll forget the who of the defense, the why of the prosecution, the headlines, the dirty accusations, the howling retorts;
we'll forget the hung jury, the cowboy admiral, the kidnap car, the caliber of the gun (what gun?), the mother's smirk (you know which one).

We've forgotten President Hoover who refused to declare martial law and Governor Judd who commuted the ten-year sentence required by law to an hour in his office for the killers to toast their punishment with champagne; but

tell me what must we remember?

Other Sources

Further Reading

Black, Cobey. *Hawaii Scandal*. Honolulu: Island Heritage, 2002.

Carroll, Dennis. *Massie/Kahahawai*. Dramatic stage production by Kumu Kahua Theatre. Honolulu, 2004.

Gajelonia, Gizelle. *Thirteen Ways of Looking at TheBus*. Honolulu: Tinfish Press, 2010.

Packer, Robert and Bob Thomas. *The Massie Case*. New York: Bantam Books, 1966.

Reinecke, John [anonymously]. *The Navy and the Massie-Kahahawai Case*. Honolulu: Honolulu Record, 1951.

Rosa, John P. *Local Story: The Massie-Kahahawai Case and the Culture of History*. Honolulu: University of Hawai'i Press, 2014.

Rosa, John P. "Local Story: The Massie Case and the Cultural Production of Local Identity in Hawai'i," *Amerasia* Journal 26:2 (2000): 93–115.

Stannard, David E. *Honor Killing: How the Infamous "Massie Affair" Transformed Hawai'i*. New York: Penguin Group, 2005.

Van Slingerland, Peter. *Something Terrible Has Happened*. New York: Harper & Row, 1966.

Wright, Theon. *Rape in Paradise*. New York: Hawthorn Books, 1966.

Viewing and Listening

Blood and Orchids. Television miniseries. Directed by Jerry Thorpe. Teleplay by Norman Katov. Lorimar Productions, 1986. Aired on CBS, February 23–24, 1986, in two 2-hour segments.

A Crime to Remember. Television Episode, Season Four. Discovery Channel. Craig Howes, Jon Kamakawiwoʻole Osorio, and John Rosa, interviewees. To be aired in 2017.

Honolulu Civil Beat and PRX Radio, Season One, Episodes 1–10, October–December 2016. "'Offshore' Podcast: Hawaii's Not Always Paradise." Available at http://feeds.civilbeat.org/civilbeatoffshore.

Zwonitzer, Mark (dir.). *The Massie Affair.* [DVD]. WGBH Boston, American Experience series, 2005.

Online Materials / Sources

The Massie Affair. Companion website to American Experience documentary. Available at http://www.pbs.org/wgbh/amex/massie/filmmore/fr.html.

Rosa, John. "The Legacy of the Massie-Kahahawai Case, 80 Years On." *Hawaii Independent.* January 8, 2012. Available at http://hawaiiindependent.net/ story/the-legacy-of-the-massie-kahahawai-case-80-years-on.

Stannard, David. "The Massie Case: Injustice and Courage." *The Honolulu Advertiser.* October 14, 2001. Available at http://the.honoluluadvertiser.com/article/2001/ Oct/14/op/op03a.html.

University of Minnesota Law Library, Clarence Darrow Digital Collection. "The Massie Trial." Available at http://darrow.law.umn.edu/trials.php?tid=5.

About the Authors

Ann Inoshita was born and raised on Oʻahu. She has a book of poems, *Mānoa Stream* (Kahuaomānoa Press), and she co-authored *No Choice but to Follow*, a book and CD of linked poems (Bamboo Ridge Press). Her short play, *Wea I Stay: A Play in Hawaiʻi*, was included in *The Statehood Project* performed by Kumu Kahua Theatre and published by Fat Ulu Productions. Her creative works have been anthologized widely in local and international journals. She teaches at Leeward Community College.

Juliet S. Kono is the author of several books: *Hilo Rains*, *Tsunami Years*, *Hoʻolulu Park and the Pepsodent Smile*, *The Bravest Opihi*, *No Choice but to Follow*, and *Anshū*, a novel. She has appeared in many anthologies and collections and is the recipient of several awards. She is retired and lives with her husband in Honolulu.

Christy Passion is a critical care nurse and poet. Her singular works have appeared in various local journals and anthologies, as well as in mainland and international journals such as *Crab Creek Review*, *Haight Ashbury Literary Journal*, *Blue Collar Review*, and *Mauri Ola*. She has received the James A. Vaughn Award for Poetry, the *Atlanta Review* International Merit Award, and the Academy of American Poetry Award. She co-authored *No Choice but to Follow* and her début collection of poetry, *Still Out of Place*, was published in 2016. She works and resides in Honolulu.

John P. Rosa is Associate Professor of History at the University of Hawaiʻi at Mānoa. He is the author of *Local Story: The Massie-Kahahawai Case and the Culture of History* (University of Hawaiʻi Press, 2014). He was raised in Kaimukī and Kāneʻohe on the island of Oʻahu.

Jean Yamasaki Toyama is professor emerita of French and former Associate Dean of the College of Languages, Linguistics and Literature at the University of Hawaiʻi at Mānoa. Her latest books include a volume of poetry, *Prepositions*, and one of short stories, *The Piano Tuner's Wife*. She is a Beckett scholar.

Acknowledgements

Any undertaking like ours is never done alone, even though we poets may have thought of ourselves as being alone. This effort is a communal one, one accomplished through the efforts of many people. First of all we wish to thank the Bamboo Ridge Press 'ohana, especially Marie Hara, Wing Tek Lum, Gail N. Harada, Joy Kobayashi-Cintrón, and Normie Salvador. Our moving deadlines and changes were always met with good humor and good will.

We must thank our book designer, Jui-Lien Sanderson, for our handsome cover and the look and feel that we sought for our work. We are grateful to John P. Rosa for his introduction and all our consultations and for providing a comprehensive timeline and list of resources. As for the items on the cover, we thank Patricia Lee for her green dress and Eddie Croom for his research in the Honolulu Police Department Museum and for use of items from their files. Many thanks to Mary Cooke, Jennifer Leung, and the Mānoa Heritage Center for their help with our research. We thank Lena Kaulia and Earle Furusato, Executive Director of Palama Settlement, who helped give authenticity to our cover, as did Troy Kimura and Victoria Nihi of the Hawai'i State Archives. We are very grateful for their assistance. Thank you to Kalihi Valley District Park for their help with the boxing gloves. We especially thank George F. Lee, photo editor of the *Honolulu Star-Advertiser*, for permission to use pictures from the newspaper's archives to give us a sense of the events of the past.

We must remember Bamboo Ridge Press for its encouragement, counsel, and belief in our book through these long years. And of course we thank them for finding the funds necessary to realize this publication. In this respect we cannot forget the Hawai'i Council for the Humanities (HCH), which through several partnership grants provided support of our publication. Moreover, along with the Sidney Stern Memorial Trust, HCH has enabled us to engage with the teachers and students of Hawai'i schools with workshops and readings through our BOGO project.